The New Caucasus

CHATHAM HOUSE PAPERS

A Russia and Eurasia Programme Publication
Programme Head: Dr Roy Allison

The Royal Institute of International Affairs, at Chatham House in London, has provided an impartial forum for discussion and debate on current international issues for nearly 80 years. Its resident research fellows, specialized information resources, and range of publications, conferences, and meetings span the fields of international politics, economics, and security. The Institute is independent of government.

Chatham House Papers are short monographs on current policy problems which have been commissioned by the RIIA. In preparing the papers, authors are advised by a study group of experts convened by the RIIA, and publication of a paper indicates that the Institute regards it as an authoritative contribution to the public debate. The Institute does not, however, hold opinions of its own; the views expressed in this publication are the responsibility of the author.

CHATHAM HOUSE PAPERS

The New Caucasus
Armenia, Azerbaijan and Georgia

Edmund Herzig

THE ROYAL INSTITUTE
OF INTERNATIONAL
AFFAIRS

CASSELL PLC

Pinter
A Cassell imprint
Wellington House, 125 Strand, London WC2R 0BB
370 Lexington Avenue, New York, NY 10017-6550

First published in 1999

British Library Cataloguing-in-Publication Data
A CIP catalogue record for this book is available from the British Library.

Library of Congress Cataloging-in-Publication Data
A CIP catalogue record for this book is available from the Library of Congress.

ISBN 1-85567-553-6 (paperback)
       1-85567-552-8 (hardback)

Typeset by Koinonia Limited
Printed and bound in Great Britain by
Biddles Limited, Guildford and King's Lynn

Contents

Contents

Acknowledgments

For help in researching and writing this paper I am indebted to more people than can individually be thanked here. Specialists, officials (in particular in the Armenian, Azerbaijani and Georgian embassies in London) and staff of NGOs and IFIs have all been generous with help, information and ideas. I have benefitted especially from conversations with Jonathan Aves, Marina Kurkchiyan, Thierry Malleret, Anna Matveeva, Gia Nodia, Willy Olsen, Armen Sarkissian and Jonathan Walters.

I am grateful to the participants of a study group, held at Chatham House to discuss a first draft of the paper, for their useful criticisms and suggestions; also to Bruno Coppieters, Peter Duncan, George Hewitt, David Miller, Razmik Panossian and Peter Roland for their written comments on the draft. Colleagues at the RIIA have given help, advice and support throughout the project. Roy Allison (Russia and Eurasia Programme), Mary Bone (Library), and Margaret May (Publications Department) have each made a special contribution to bringing the work to publication.

Like many other students of the contemporary Caucasus, I owe special thanks to Liz Fuller for her reporting and analysis of developments in the region, published by RFE/RL and OMRI.

February 1999   E.H.

Abbreviations

AIOC	Azerbaijan International Operating Company
ANA	Armenian National Army
ANM	Armenian (Pan-)National Movement
APF	Azerbaijani Popular Front
ARF	Armenian Revolutionary Federation (or Dashnaktsutiun)
BSEC	Black Sea Economic Cooperation
CFE	Conventional Forces in Europe
CIS	Commonwealth of Independent States
CSCE/ OSCE	Conference on (subsequently Organisation for) Security and Cooperation in Europe
CUG	Citizens' Union of Georgia
EBRD	European Bank for Reconstruction and Development
ECO	Economic Cooperation Organization
FSU	Former Soviet Union
GUAM	Georgia, Ukraine, Azerbaijan, Moldova
IDP	internally displaced person
IFI	international financial institution
IMF	International Monetary Fund
JCC	Joint Control Commission
OIC	Organization of Islamic Conference
OMRI	Open Media Research Institute
PfP	Partnership for Peace
PKF	peace-keeping force
SOCAR	Azerbaijani state oil company
TRACECA	Transport Corridor Europe–Caucasus–Asia
UNDP	United Nations Development Programme
UN/ECE	United Nations, Economic Commission for Europe
WTO	World Trade Organization

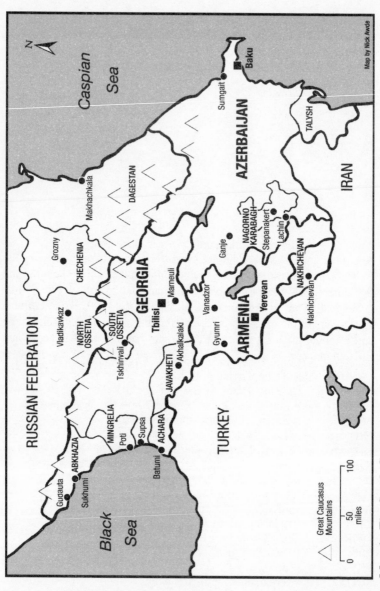

Map 1: The South Caucasus

Chapter 1

Introduction

The 'new' in the title of this study requires some explanation, since the Caucasus mountains are, at the risk of tautology, as old as the hills, and the time frame here employed is human and historical rather than geological. What is new for the Caucasus in the 1990s is the political sovereignty of the three former Soviet republics of Armenia, Azerbaijan and Georgia, the dismantling of the Soviet barriers that had kept them isolated in a remote corner of the USSR, their adoption of new political and economic systems, and the post-Soviet configuration of international forces that surround them. The subject, as given in the subtitle, is confined to Armenia, Azerbaijan and Georgia (which collectively are often referred to from a Russocentric perspective as Transcaucasia, but here will be called the South Caucasus). The North Caucasus region will be touched on only in so far as it impinges on developments in the three independent states of the South Caucasus.

Geography and history

The Caucasus region marks the meeting point of the Eurasian steppe to the north and the Middle Eastern highlands, comprising the Anatolian and Iranian plateaux, to the south. The surrounding mountain ranges (the Taurus and Zagros to the southwest, the Elbruz to the southeast and the main Caucasus ridge to the north) and the Black and Caspian Seas to west and east have over millennia acted less to obstruct than to channel human movement across the South Caucasus, so that in spite of its mountains and uplands the geography of the South Caucasus may be characterized

1

as open and accessible, at least relative to the more formidable mountain barriers around it.

This geographical configuration underlies the historical significance of the South Caucasus as a borderland and bridge between civilizations and peoples. Legend places the earthly paradise and the resting place of Noah's ark here, reflecting the land's attractiveness for human settlement, and migration has brought many peoples to and through the South Caucasus, leaving a mosaic of ethnic communities speaking a bewildering variety of Caucasian, Indo-European and Turkic languages. If diversity is the predominant characteristic of the region's demographic composition, its cultural character is defined by its bridging role between civilizations based in Mesopotamia to the south, the Anatolian plateau to the west, Iran to the southeast and Russia and the Eurasian steppe to the north. A true melting-pot for the many cultural currents that have flowed in from all around, the South Caucasus possesses distinctive, if not uniform, characteristics in its popular and material culture, characteristics which overarch the ethnic, linguistic and religious diversity of its peoples.

The region's economic significance has derived partly from its openness to traffic in transit on the overland routes of continental trade, partly from its products and resources: throughout history, raw silk, cotton and other agricultural products, as well as craft manufactures, have been exported from here, and its upland pastures have attracted nomadic pastoralists.

The political history of the South Caucasus has been turbulent. Ethnic diversity, weakness relative to the empires of the Middle East and the steppe, a strategic location at the meeting point of those empires, tempting economic resources and trade routes, and openness to the passage of armies as well as merchants' caravans have combined to keep the region fragmented and to make it a favourite battleground for neighbouring powers. Romans and Persians, Arabs and Byzantines, the successor khanates of Genghis Khan's Mongol empire, and the Ottoman Turkish and the Safavi Iranian empires have all contested control of the South Caucasus, with the region changing hands and being partitioned and repartitioned with startling frequency. Some of these wars and invasions have been so destructive and disruptive as to cause long-term shifts in the region's demographic and economic balance.

The view of the region's history as one of continuous foreign invasion and occupation must, however, be tempered by recognition that there were periods, albeit rather few and short-lived, when independent kingdoms and autonomous principalities were established in Georgia and Armenia and on the territory that is now Azerbaijan (though the geographers and historians of the past mostly used other names to describe it – Caucasian Albania, Arran, Shirvan, for example). Moreover, the ancient and medieval empires that held sway over the South Caucasus were founded not on national but on dynastic ideologies. They were multi-ethnic and often allowed the Caucasian peoples to participate in their political, cultural and economic lives. Discrimination was more frequently based on sectarian than on ethnic criteria. Thus in certain periods Armenians played important roles in the Byzantine, Safavi and Ottoman empires, while in the Islamic empires the Muslim peoples of the South Caucasus were generally on equal terms with other Muslims. Caucasian elites sought to exploit the international balance of power to further their own ambitions. The linkage of local, regional and international dynamics is a persistent characteristic of Caucasian politics.

By the early nineteenth century, Tsarist Russia gained control of the South Caucasus and retained that control until the 1991 collapse of the Soviet Union, with a brief interlude of Caucasian independence and intervention by other foreign powers between 1917 and 1921. The external borders of the region as we see it today were defined by Russia's Caucasian wars of conquest and subsequently revised by treaties with Turkey signed in the early Soviet period. Its internal borders – delimiting the territories of Armenia, Azerbaijan and Georgia and of the autonomous republics and regions incorporated in them – are a product of Tsarist administrative divisions adjusted to fit the nationalities policy and political requirements of the Soviet government of the 1920s and 1930s.

Nearly two centuries of Russian rule produced a deep impact on the Caucasus. Tsarist and particularly Soviet government was much more thoroughgoing and far-reaching than that of the earlier empires. It produced demographic changes that tended to concentrate ethnic populations within defined territorial homelands. It accelerated the region's economic and social development, and shaped the Caucasian peoples' national identities and nationalist consciousness, which burgeoned partly in response to the deliberate stimulus of Moscow's nationalities policies, and partly in reaction against Russian domination. The Soviet regime also deliberately curtailed the region's relations with its southern and western neighbours. The seven decades of Soviet rule thus contradicted the region's fundamental geographical openness and form an exception to its historical bridging role.

The Caucasus today

The demise of the Soviet Union restored independence to Armenia, Azerbaijan and Georgia. It allowed their governments and peoples to choose their political and economic systems, and to re-establish political, economic and human relations with their neighbours and the wider international community. The attainment of independence gave rise to euphoria among Armenians, Azeris and Georgians and to hopes of a free and prosperous future, released from the twin yokes of Russian-communist domination and the failed Soviet command economy.

The Soviet collapse also left them, however, poorly equipped to take advantage of this opportunity. Neither political institutions and elites nor economic resources and infrastructure were ready for the challenges of independence. Even culturally and territorially, one could argue, the three republics lacked a solid foundation for independence, since the national consciousness among all the Caucasian peoples was characteri-zed by a high degree of exclusivity and antagonism towards other peoples (especially those who inhabited the same territory), while the distribution of territory among the states was contested between governments and peoples. Constitutionally, the new states were not fully fledged, since the transition from the pseudo-federal Soviet system to a nation-states system left the status of the Soviet ethno-territorial autonomies in limbo, giving rise to bitter conflicts even before the break-up of the Soviet Union. These handicaps led pessimists to predict the early collapse of one or more of the newly independent states, or at best their rapid reversion to subordinate status in Russia's or some other regional power's empire or sphere of influence.

Will either of these predictions prove to be correct? Is Caucasian independence a sustainable reality in the post-Soviet world order, or is it a transient phenomenon symptomatic of temporary Russian weakness? The answers to these questions are of interest not only to the peoples of the Caucasus and their neighbours, but to a wide circle of policy-makers, business people and students, specialists, journalists and enthusiasts whose interests have become engaged in the region.

Nearly a decade after the momentous events of 1991 it is possible to identify some of the trends and dynamics that will decide the answers to these questions. This study uses primary sources and the extensive secondary literature which has been generated in the past six or seven years to analyse the trajectory and sustainability of developments in the Caucasus. It employs a comparative method to look for shared patterns in the three countries and to question the likelihood of the development of common interests and regional cooperation.

Chapter 2 focuses on political development and the twin processes of nation- and state-building to examine the balance between ethnic and civic criteria for establishing national communities, and to question whether the Caucasian states yet possess political institutions capable of sustaining state sovereignty and national cohesion. It assesses progress in the development of democracy, of new legitimizing ideologies, and of civil society.

The region's conflicts and the other security challenges confronting its governments are the subject of Chapter 3. Special consideration is given to the factors that sparked and fuelled the conflicts and to those that affect the prospects for their resolution.

In Chapter 4 the new international environment is analysed in terms of the factors that are shaping the interests and policies of the Caucasian states, and of regional and extra-regional actors. The chapter also assesses the achievements of the Caucasian states' foreign policies, and questions whether the post-Soviet world order will break the historical pattern of brief periods of Caucasian independence truncated by conflictual great power intervention.

Chapter 5 examines economic change and performance in the Caucasus, assessing whether the Caucasian economies, with their small markets and limited resources, can survive in the modern world economic system. It considers the region's ability to attract foreign investment and the possible consequences for Azerbaijan and the region as a whole of the development of Caspian oil and gas. The prospects for the realization of plans to establish the South Caucasus as a transit corridor for east–west and north–south trade are discussed. The chapter focuses also on the social impact of economic change, questioning whether the Caucasian economies will be able to provide even the most basic needs of their peoples.

In conclusion, Chapter 6 highlights trends and dynamics for stability in Armenia, Azerbaijan and Georgia, and identifies key priorities for the medium-term development of the South Caucasus region.

Chapter 2

Politics

The last decade of politics in Armenia, Azerbaijan and Georgia has been dominated by nation- and state-building. These processes began prior to the collapse of the Soviet Union and remain far from complete. Nation-building has required the attempt to define and consolidate political communities – to decide who belongs and who is excluded – and to articulate their relations with other political communities, including those laying claim to the same territories. State-building has centred on the establishment of viable government institutions capable of controlling and administering key resources (territory, coercive power, wealth) and of sustaining themselves beyond the political lives of individual office-holders. These processes underlie the flux of Caucasian politics, with its rapidly shifting and unpredictable power struggles and ideological currents, its moments of euphoria (the attainment of independence), and despair (at military defeat and impotence in the face of powerful enemies), and its current normal tenor of cynicism, frustration and disillusionment (at the betrayal of ideals, and at the failure of 'democracy' to deliver what was hoped and of today's leaders to do better than yesterday's in living up to their promises). This chapter analyses the underlying political dynamics in the three Caucasian states, examines their points of similarity and difference, and assesses the prospects for the nation- and state-building processes.

Nationalism in the Caucasus

In all three Caucasian countries today's politics have developed out of the late Soviet period politics which pitted national independence movements against local communist elites and the ultimate authority of Moscow. In the late 1980s dissident nationalists found the new freedoms of glasnost and perestroika. These, and the communists' loss of ideological conviction and political will, gave nationalists the opportunity to mobilize mass popular support. Caucasian nationalist movements shared many of the characteristics of their counterparts in the Baltic region and other Soviet republics: rejection of colonial or imperial rule from Moscow, assertion of the primacy of their national language and culture (as against the Russian language and super-national Soviet culture), and resistance to Moscow's economic exploitation and environmental degradation of the motherland. But in the Caucasus the nationalist discourse was concerned not only with relations with Russia and Moscow, but also – and no less acutely – with other issues concerning each nation's history and its relations with its neighbours and with the various peoples inhabiting its territory.

Growing out of intellectual traditions (which date back to the eighteenth century or beyond in the case of the Armenians, to the nineteenth century in that of the Georgians and to as late as the early twentieth century for the Azeris), the nationalism of the Caucasian peoples was tempered by seventy years of Soviet government, whose ambivalent nationality policy on the one hand consolidated and popularized the concept of historically validated exclusive national territories – the fifteen union republics of the USSR, and the subordinate autonomous republics, regions (*oblasts*) and areas (*okrugs*) within them – and promoted the development of official national cultural institutions and expression (academies of sciences, universities, theatres, operas, writers' unions, publishing houses, sanitized folk arts, etc.), while on the other it suppressed nationalist expression that overstepped a shifting dividing line between the tolerated and the dissident by challenging the ideological and political bases of the Soviet regime, or even questioning the desirability of incorporation in the Russian empire. Dissident intellectuals (artists and academics) faced severe penalties, but became underground heroes to their own ethnic communities.

By the end of the Soviet period, some degree of national consciousness was universal in the Caucasian republics, and many, especially the better educated, privately held much stronger nationalist opinions than they dared to express openly. With hindsight, it is easy to see the potential for mass mobilization. Three particular characteristics of Caucasian nationalism were important in shaping the trajectory of the region's political development.[1]

Russian domination

Desire for full independence and resentment of 'Russian' Soviet rule was shared by Armenians, Azerbaijanis and Georgians. All remembered that in the aftermath of the Russian Revolution their republics had enjoyed a brief independence that was brought to an end by Bolshevik conquest. In Georgia and Azerbaijan there was a much stronger sense of resentment of Russian rule than in Armenia, where regret for the loss of independence was tempered by a kinder view of Russia's historical role as protector from the Turkish menace. All Caucasians were conscious of Slavic prejudices against them (as dark-skinned and as black marketeers), which were only partly offset by sympathy among the Russian intelligentsia for the Christian Georgians and Armenians, with their ancient 'civilized' cultures. Azeris, like other Muslim Soviet nationalities, were aware that the Soviet regime had a special aversion to Islam, and that there was widespread prejudice against Muslims among the Slavic peoples.

Unfinished territorial business

Dissatisfaction with the Soviet territorial division of the 1920s that established the borders of the three union republics and their autonomies was another common theme. Armenians, most of all, felt that they had been the losers in the carve-up of the Caucasus. Nationalists believed that not only Karabagh (an autonomous region of Azerbaijan) but also Nakhichevan (an autonomous republic of Azerbaijan) were historically Armenian land, and that Armenia had lost out in other ways in the demarcation of borders with both Georgia and Azerbaijan. The lands 'lost' to Georgia and Azerbaijan formed a small part of the Armenian *irredenta*, which lay mainly in western Armenia/Turkey. These irredentist claims, together with the demand for recognition of the 1915 Genocide, lie at the heart of the 'Armenian Cause' (*Hay dat*), and any concession on them is widely perceived as a national betrayal. The most territorially dispersed and cosmopolitan of the peoples of the Caucasus, Armenians were also conscious that national delimitation had deprived them of what had in the nineteenth century been their major cultural and commercial centres: Tiflis/Tbilisi, Shushi/Shusha and Baku.

In Georgia resentments focused less on territories disputed with the other republics than on the autonomies, particularly Abkhazia and South Ossetia, that were viewed as having been planted by Moscow to vitiate Georgian aspirations to nationhood, a view which readily fed into distrust of the Abkhaz and Ossetes (and other minority peoples) as Moscow's agents.

In Azerbaijan dissatisfaction with internal Soviet territorial arrangements was less of an issue, though Azeri nationalists laid historic claim to
Zangezur (the mountainous southern region of Armenia that separates
Azerbaijan from Nakhichevan) and viewed the border definition as
deliberate divide-and-rule manipulation by Moscow. They also felt they
had a claim to the Azeri-populated Marneuli district in Georgia. Rather, it
was the separation of the Azeri people and historical Azerbaijan by the
border with Iran (established in 1828) that constituted the main territorial
grievance. Like the Georgians, Azeri nationalists viewed the existence of
an autonomous territorial entity (Karabagh) within their republic as an
artificial lever installed by Moscow to facilitate Russian manipulation of
regional politics and to frustrate Azeri national aspirations.

The minority populations also had their territorial grievances, though
these were mainly directed against the republics' majority populations
and administrations. The Karabagh Armenians believed that in the 1920s
their territory should have been incorporated into Armenia rather than
Azerbaijan. The South Ossetes desired unification with North Ossetia in
a single Ossetian homeland. The Abkhaz rejected their territory's 1931
incorporation into Georgia as an autonomous republic (between 1921
and 1931 Abkhazia had not been subordinate to Tbilisi's authority).
Those minority nationalities that had been denied ethnic homelands in
the Soviet territorial delimitation, among them the Lezgins inhabiting
both sides of the border separating Azerbaijan and Dagestan, resented the
failure to recognize their rights to an ethnic territory.

Language and culture
Nationalists among all the Caucasian peoples accused their rulers of
denying them full expression of their cultural aspirations and seeking to
erode national identities. Language was a particularly sensitive issue.
Georgians, Armenians and Azeris all felt that their languages and
cultures were threatened by a tacit policy of Russification and assimilation into a homogenized Soviet people. The defence of the language and
the preservation of national cultural monuments and traditions were a
major focus of nationalist energies. In Armenia there was an additional
focus on overcoming Soviet constraints on support for the Armenian
cause shared with the diaspora Armenian communities.

Again, these grievances were directed not solely towards Moscow and
Russia, but towards all those forces which frustrated free national-
cultural expression. Thus for Armenians the cultural rights of the inner
diaspora in the Soviet Union, especially in Azerbaijan and Georgia, were

an important focus, while for Azeris it was the rights of Azeris in Armenia, Georgia, Dagestan and Iran.

Among the minorities similar concerns about the preservation of language, culture and identity were no less strongly felt, but here the threat emanated not from Moscow but from the union republics. Karabagh Armenians accused Baku of denying their cultural rights and seeking to assimilate or expel them, the Abkhaz levelled similar accusations against Tbilisi, and so forth. In addition, the minorities considered themselves discriminated against in other ways, from denial of career opportunities, to ethnic bias in the allocation of economic resources among regions, to incidents of public abuse or hostility.

While open expression of these resentments and grievances was more or less repressed, nationalist intellectuals found ways to get their message across, ranging from the outright dissidence of *samizdat* publication to seemingly innocuous and abstruse academic or cultural works whose contents, however, advanced nationalist claims that were transparent to their intended audiences. Georgian and Armenian art historians hotly debated the minutest points of medieval architecture in order to establish exclusive national claims on monasteries and churches, and by extension the towns and regions in which they are located. Armenian and Azeri philologists and palaeographers crossed swords over the extinct Caucasian Albanian language, while their historians endlessly disputed the region's historical demography, all in the struggle to establish exclusive claims on Karabagh (and other territories). Similar disputes raged between Georgian and Abkhaz academics.

Thus by the late 1980s, in spite of the omnipresent Soviet slogan of the 'friendship between peoples', in spite of the reality of often harmonious relations between individuals and communities of different ethnic groups, and of intermarriage across ethnic lines (though this was less prevalent in the Caucasus than in other Soviet republics),[2] the battle-lines for the national liberation struggles, and for the conflicts within and between the Caucasian republics, were already clearly drawn. Nationalist militants knew the obstacles and enemies that stood between them and the realization of their agendas. These battle-lines pitted the three main south Caucasian peoples not only against the Soviet regime and Russian rule, but also in varying degrees against one another, and against the union republics' minority nationalities, especially those in possession of autonomous territories.

The struggle for independence

As a result of these characteristic features, far from being a straight fight between Armenian, Azerbaijani and Georgian nationalists and the Soviet centre, the independence struggle in the South Caucasus was complex and multi-faceted, though tending inexorably to the increasingly forceful articulation and pursuit of national aspirations and demands by all parties.

The start of the process can be dated to February 1988, when the regional council (*soviet*) of Karabagh voted to transfer from Azerbaijan to Armenia, posing the first major nationalist challenge to Gorbachev's policies. At this stage nationalists in both Karabagh and Armenia still saw themselves as loyal Soviet citizens, and appealed to Moscow to realize their aspirations. They believed their demand to uphold the Karabagh Armenians' democratic choice and undo the territorial injustice inflicted by Stalin was in full harmony with the aims of glasnost and perestroika, and Gorbachev's rejection of the Stalinist heritage.[3] In the first instance their quarrel was inter- and intra-republican, pitting Armenians in Karabagh and Armenia against the Azerbaijani Soviet authorities and, after the massacre of Armenians in Sumgait at the end of February 1988, against Azeris in general. It was only gradually, and especially after July 1988 when Moscow definitively rejected their demands, that the Armenian national movement began to take on the character of an independence movement, voicing the entire dissident agenda, from democratization to environmental issues. A group of committed intellectuals, singled out by their nationalist credentials, determination, organizational capacity or gift for public speaking, assumed the leadership of this movement, forming the Karabagh Committee.

In Azerbaijan too the Karabagh issue was the catalyst for the emergence of a mass national movement.[4] Vociferous Armenian demands, which found sympathetic echoes in some Russian and Western media, evoked an Azerbaijani response. This not only advanced counter-arguments against the Armenian claims, but gave vent to the whole range of Azeri national issues. As in Armenia, dissatisfaction with Moscow's handling of the Karabagh issue and the perception of Russian bias played a decisive role in transforming an originally uncoordinated and disparate group of actors into the Azerbaijani Popular Front (APF), a mass movement coalescing around the cause of national independence, while voicing a wide range of concerns spanning cultural rights, democratization and economic exploitation. In 'Black January' 1990 Soviet security

11

forces used rioting and a further massacre of Armenians in Baku as the pretext for a brutal suppression of the APF, killing at least 120 civilians and forcing the movement underground. In the aftermath the APF grew increasingly radical, with some of its more moderate members splitting to form their own group.

In Georgia there was no single cause which mobilized nationalist opposition, but a number of separate issues emerged as focal points for a gathering confrontation between the communist authorities and an opposition that never fully united under a single umbrella organization or movement. One such issue was a plan to build a new railway linking Georgia and Russia which nationalists believed too damaging to the environment and to Georgian cultural monuments. Another was the revelation that Soviet troops were using an ancient monastery for artillery practice.[5] Public concern over alleged discrimination against ethnic Georgians in Abkhazia and South Ossetia, and more generally over the threat to the Georgian nation posed by minorities (Azeri and Armenian as well as Abkhaz and Ossete), engendered an increasingly heated public debate, in which nationalists castigated Soviet disregard for national rights. By March 1989 the political situation was extremely tense, with the Abkhaz issue coming to centre stage, as calls from Abkhazia for the restoration of Union Republic status elicited a strong reaction in Georgia. From denial of the Abkhaz demands, Georgian protesters progressed to voicing their own demands for independence. On 9 April Soviet troops attacked peaceful demonstrators in Tbilisi, killing nineteen, injuring hundreds and causing a deep polarization between the communist government and the opposition, as well as helping the more radical elements of the opposition to seize the initiative.

In all three republics, within a period of months in 1988–9 mass national movements emerged to challenge the legitimacy of Soviet power and advance nationalist demands that rapidly crystallized as articulated political agendas, rather than heterogeneous lists of cultural or other grievances. In all three the nationalist opposition mobilized mass support through demonstrations and strikes, a 'street' democracy that participants felt more vital and legitimate than the 'paper' constitutional democracy of the Soviet political system.[6] The course of political developments in each republic, however, was shaped in large part by the different responses of the republican communist authorities to the specific national challenge.

Armenia is the most ethnically homogeneous of the Caucasian states and contains no ethno-territorial autonomies. These characteristics created a much more favourable background for the emergence of some degree of national consensus. Even among members of the communist elite, there was a considerable degree of sympathy for much of the nationalist agenda; this undermined the Soviet republican government's ability to offer effective ideological or political resistance to the nationalists. The authorities early on attempted to coopt part of the nationalist agenda (as early as June 1988 the Armenian Supreme Soviet – under intense public pressure – supported the Karabagh Soviet's call for unification with Armenia), but were always in a reactive position, the initiative resting with the highly motivated and articulate Karabagh Committee and its campaign of mass demonstrations and strikes.

The one serious attempt at suppression backfired: when the members of the Karabagh Committee were arrested and imprisoned in December 1988, it only further galvanized public political activism and weakened the communists' claim to be a national government. After the release of the Karabagh Committee members in May 1989 there was a progressive process of dialogue, cooperation and transfer of power from the communists to the nationalists. This process is clearly demonstrated in the profile of the Armenian National Movement (ANM), the new opposition political vehicle established in September 1989. It included many Communist Party members and, once in government following victory in protracted parliamentary elections in spring–summer 1990, it distributed some ministerial portfolios to members of the old communist elite.[7] Something like a national consensus emerged to back the ANM government at the time of its most intense confrontation with Moscow (late summer 1990 to August 1991) – an important factor in its ability to survive this period and a good foundation for a stable transition to independence. In a referendum in September 1991 Armenians voted 94 per cent in favour of independence and the following month Ter-Petrosian was elected president with 83 per cent of the votes cast.

In Azerbaijan, the communist authorities, led by Ayaz Mutalibov, adopted the opposite tactic. Taking advantage of the January 1990 suppression of the APF, Mutalibov attempted to seize the political initiative by using the support of the Soviet centre to crush the Karabagh rebellion and demonstrate that the Azerbaijani communist authorities represented the best hope for achieving national goals, reform and stability. Ultimately Mutalibov's bid to ride out the nationalist opposition with Moscow's support was undone by events in Moscow, where the rapid collapse of communist power after the failed August 1991 coup (for which Mutalibov had rashly expressed support) deprived him of his main

13

prop. Though he won the September presidential election (as the sole candidate) and renounced his communist past, the damage to his political credibility was irreparable. In November 1991 mass demonstrations forced the communist-dominated Supreme Soviet to dissolve itself and establish an unelected fifty-seat National Council in its place. The seats were divided equally between former communist supporters of Mutalibov and the APF. The loss of Moscow's support also left Mutalibov without the coercive instruments to bring Karabagh to heel. The conflict eventually cost him the presidency, with the massacre of Azeri civilians in Khojali in February 1992 forcing his resignation. In May of the same year parliamentary manoeuvres intended to restore him to the presidency instead gave the APF the chance to oust him in a bloodless *coup d'état*. The APF's hold on power was confirmed and legitimized by the victory of Abulfaz Elchibey in a presidential election the following month (though the unelected National Assembly remained the sole legislature until the November 1995 parliamentary election). The polarization and lack of dialogue between the communists and the nationalists, the splits and disunity in both camps, and the violent and erratic political process leading up to the nationalists' victory, present a sharp contrast to Armenia and provided a weak basis for nascent independent political development.

Georgia's road to independence followed a third course. Though the communist authorities made significant concessions to nationalist demands as early as 1988, and in 1991 made a last-ditch attempt to coopt a large part of the nationalist agenda, they never succeeded in entering into the kind of dialogue with the opposition that had allowed compromise and consensus to emerge in Armenia. In part this may be attributed to the more fragmented nature of the Georgian opposition and the more radical character of its most prominent leaders, notably Zviad Gamsakhurdia. The shooting of demonstrators in Tbilisi in April 1989 robbed the communist authorities of any real possibility of presenting themselves as a credible national government and ruled out compromise with the opposition. In spite of pursuing a strong nationalist policy programme from April 1989 to autumn 1990, the communists were heavily defeated in a parliamentary election in October 1990. The outright winner, with 155 of the 250 seats, was Gamsakhurdia's radical Round Table–Free Georgia bloc; the Communist Party came a poor second with 64 seats. More moderate nationalist groupings failed to make an impact in the election, while parties representing the interests of regional and ethnic minorities had been excluded at the registration stage. In marked contrast to the Armenian parliament elected a few months earlier, the new Georgian parliament was highly polarized, with the nationalists now in the driving seat and the communists an unreconciled opposition. Georgia declared its independence on 9 April 1991, and the following month Gamsakhurdia won 87 per cent of the vote in a presidential election, completing the victory of the radical nationalists.

In conclusion, marked differences in the character and breadth of appeal of the Armenian, Azerbaijani and Georgian nationalist movements, in the responses of the republican and Moscow communist authorities and in the unfolding of events account for the political configurations in the three republics at the threshold of independence. In all three republics the communist regime ultimately lacked the ideological conviction or political strength (especially after the communist collapse in Moscow) to mount an effective defence of its power, but the speed and readiness of the communists to recognize their defeat differed significantly between the republics. In both Azerbaijan and Georgia the killing of civilians by Soviet troops played a major role in radicalizing the opposition and reducing the possibilities for political compromise.

Regime consolidation

The immediate political challenge facing the new independent governments was to consolidate their control over their territories and their states' coercive and material resources.[8] The strength or weakness of the political basis laid down during the run-up to independence was a crucial factor in the success or failure of the first months and years of independent state-building, with Armenia enjoying a far more stable transition than Azerbaijan or Georgia. Moreover, the same factors that had favoured Armenia over its neighbours prior to independence (ethnic homogeneity, and the absence of ethno-territorial autonomies and ongoing conflict in its territory) continued to work to its advantage.

Territory

At the time of independence the Yerevan authorities were in control of the whole of the republic of Armenia. The collapse of the Soviet regime had severely weakened central authority at republic as well as all-Union level, but no regional or ethnic forces had emerged to contest the territorial integrity of the Armenian republic. The new constitution adopted in 1995 further reinforced the capital's control over the regions by introducing a system of local government based on ten large districts (*marz*), each headed by a governor enjoying wide powers and appointed from Yerevan.

In Azerbaijan and Georgia, by contrast, there were ongoing wars as the republican, now national, governments struggled and failed to frustrate the secessionist ambitions of the ethno-territorial autonomies in Karabagh, Abkhazia and South Ossetia (see Chapter 3). Other regional or ethnic demands further impaired Tbilisi's and Baku's ability to control the whole territory of the republics of Georgia and Azerbaijan (notably in Achara and Samtskhe-Javakheti in Georgia and over the Lezgin and Talysh issues in Azerbaijan).[9]

The failure to establish and maintain their states' territorial integrity has remained an acute weakness for successive governments in Tbilisi and Baku, since this is a prerequisite for the legitimacy of any government. National constitutional and administrative structures cannot be finalized before settlements to conflicts are negotiated. Apart from Karabagh and the other territories lost to the Armenians, however, Baku has been able to establish increasingly secure control over the rest of Azerbaijan. In Georgia that process is less advanced, with Achara and, to a lesser extent, Samtskhe-Javakheti and other regions still under the control of local elites over which Tbilisi is wary or incapable of exercising full control.

Political control over coercive force

The Soviet break-up created states that were lacking many of the necessary attributes of statehood. In the Caucasus, the embryonic state of national armed forces (common to all post-Soviet states except Russia), combined with the fact that even prior to independence the three republics found themselves embroiled in military conflicts, created a situation in which informal military structures sprang up to fight for the national cause.[10] The leaders of those informal military structures developed interests and agendas that did not always coincide with those of nascent national governments, which struggled to control them while remaining militarily dependent on them.

Again, Armenia presents a contrasting picture to Azerbaijan and Georgia. By the time the ANM took control of parliament in summer 1990, a number of militias had grown up, primarily to support the fight for Karabagh's independence. On 25 July Mikhail Gorbachev issued a decree requiring the immediate disarmament of all paramilitary groups, and thus presenting Levon Ter-Petrosian (elected chairman of the Armenian parliament on 4 August) with his first major challenge. After three weeks of mounting tension Ter-Petrosian was able to bring to heel the largest of Armenia's twenty-odd militias, the Armenian National Army (ANA).[11] Its members, like those of most other militias, were subsequently incorporated into the new national army. Political control over the army and the other security forces was consolidated through the powerful ministries of defence and the interior, which have received large shares of government spending as well as a free hand in pursuing their economic interests. The government has been able to rely on the loyalty of the security forces at moments of crisis, for example during the violent demonstration following the September 1996 presidential election, though the potential countervailing political weight of these 'power' ministries was starkly revealed in February 1998 when the defence and interior ministers joined forces with Prime Minister Robert Kocharian and the defence ministry-affiliated Yerkrapah faction in parliament to oust President Ter-Petrosian. Thus even within the state apparatus, the military and security forces have been able to develop autonomous interests and agendas, much like the paramilitaries (as well as taking over a considerable part of their economic and criminal activities), and have the capacity to act as brokers rather than instruments of political power.

In Azerbaijan the APF government came to power only in mid-1992, so it had no opportunity to establish control over defence, interior or militia forces prior to independence. The prospects for good relations with the police and interior ministry forces were far from favourable, since these were widely believed to have played a sinister role in the massacres of Armenians in Sumgait (1988) and Baku (1990) that had had such a damaging effect on international perceptions of Azerbaijan and had provided the pretext for the Soviet military intervention of 'Black January'. In the virtual absence of a national army, the main fighting role in the Karabagh war was in any case being played by militias and paramilitary groups; the brigade led by Suret Huseinov – a wealthy entrepreneur who enjoyed close links with the Russian military base in Ganje – achieved particular prominence.

President Abulfaz Elchibey cultivated links with Huseinov as a patriotic and effective commander, appointing him deputy prime minister with special powers in conducting the Karabagh war. In winter 1993, however, when the Azerbaijani forces suffered defeats in the war, Elchibey dismissed Huseinov, alienating both him and his troops. Back in his home town of Ganje, Huseinov took advantage of the Russians' withdrawal from their local base to secure the transfer of additional equipment for his private army (neither the precise nature of Huseinov's undoubtedly close links with the Russian military nor the level within the Russian military or political establishment at which the arms transfer was agreed has ever been clearly established[12]). In June 1993 he defeated a contingent sent against him by the government before marching on the capital. The military weakness of the APF government was exposed when the security and interior ministries informed Elchibey that they would not oppose Huseinov's advance, forcing him to transfer power to Heydar Aliyev.[13]

Heydar Aliyev in turn faced problems with insubordinate security forces. There were coup attempts in October 1994, March 1995 and autumn 1996, all involving disaffected elements in Azerbaijan's security forces, notably the special police units which have since been disbanded.[14] Aliyev, however, exploited successive crises to remove officials whose loyalty was suspect and to consolidate his own control over the security forces through the ministries of the interior and defence.[15]

Georgia's experience of the destabilizing political consequences of uncontrolled military units has been even more intense, leading the country to civil war and the brink of disintegration in late 1993. Zviad Gamsakhurdia, in spite of his overwhelming electoral mandate, never had reliable coercive power to support his leadership. From the outbreak of serious fighting in the South Ossetian and Abkhazian conflicts, the leading role on the Georgian side was played by paramilitary militias, which simultaneously engaged in extortion and other criminal activities. The strongest of these was Jaba Ioseliani's Mkhedrioni militia, which by late 1990 was operating quite independently of any political control. In early 1991, however, measures were taken to rectify the situation. A National Guard was established under the leadership of Tengiz Kitovani, and the Mkhedrioni were suppressed by the Georgian police with Soviet military cooperation. Ioseliani was arrested. If this presented an opportunity for establishing political control over military and security forces, Gamsakhurdia failed to seize it. Differences between him and Kitovani soon emerged, and it became clear that the National Guard's primary loyalty was to its commander rather than the president. Gamsakhurdia had allowed the creation of another militia with its own warlord, rather than a reliable, politically controlled force. In August 1991 he attempted to bring the National Guard under political control through the ministry of the interior, but instead provoked open rebellion, with Kitovani's National Guard and the Mkhedrioni under Ioseliani (who escaped from detention) joining forces to oust him in the violent coup of December 1991.[16]

The return of Eduard Shevardnadze in March 1992 to lead the new government did not alter the basic lack of loyal military and security forces at the disposal of the political leadership, though he proved far more adept in managing his relations with the various commanders. From 1992 until 1995, in order to ensure their loyalty, Shevardnadze was obliged to keep Kitovani and Ioseliani in prominent government positions – they had, after all, been instrumental in inviting him to return from Moscow, in a self-interested bid to give their regime international credibility – and to tolerate the overt criminality and lawlessness of their followers. In September 1993, shortly before the end of the Abkhazian war, Shevardnadze took control of the ministry of the interior and rebuilt his power from this base, gradually squeezing the warlords. At the same time, he was forced to call on Russian military support (at the cost of significant military and political concessions) in order to suppress the rebellion of Gamsakhurdia in Mingrelia in western Georgia.

Shevardnadze subsequently bolstered the ministries of defence, state security and the interior, appointing as ministers former officers of the KGB and the Soviet military with good connections in Russia. Gradually he was able to consolidate political control over the country's military, police and paramilitary forces. Kitovani was arrested in January 1995, the National Guard ceasing to be a threat thereafter. The Mkhedrioni were suppressed from early summer 1995. An attempt on his life in August 1995 provided the break for Shevardnadze to move even more decisively, and Ioseliani was arrested in November. It also allowed Shevardnadze to replace other senior officials in the power ministries who were suspected of too close connections with Russian security circles.[17]

It is only since 1996, therefore, that political control over coercive resources can be called secure. Even now, the presence of Russian military bases and border guards on Georgian territory and the Russian connections and suspected sympathies of many in the security establishment (notably former Defence Minister Vardiko Nadibaidze) raise questions about the real locus of military power in Georgia, while the attempt to assassinate Shevardnadze in February 1998 gave a stark reminder that the state is still far from enjoying a monopoly of armed force.

Control of economic resources and the emergence of new elites
An understanding of the formation of new elites, of the processes by which they have seized and retain control over economic resources, and of the dynamics of interaction of different subgroups and individuals within new elites is essential for identifying the prospects for medium-

term political and social stability in the Caucasian states. Yet these are subjects which remain to a large extent opaque. Reliable data are difficult or dangerous to collect, and much of what passes for information or analysis serves one or other personal or political agenda. This section is, therefore, obliged to be speculative in attempting to trace elite relationships and the interface of political and economic power.

In the Caucasus, as throughout the Soviet Union, the Soviet-era elite comprised the Communist Party, which held a monopoly of all positions of political and economic power. Advancement beyond a certain level in most careers was possible only for Communist Party members. Historical factors tended to reinforce the party's monopoly. The lack of long traditions of independence or self-rule meant there was no strong, coherent national elite in Armenia, Azerbaijan or Georgia; all had long been governed by metropolitan elites, either Russians or Russian-educated. Stalin's purges eradicated the survivors of the pre-Soviet leadership, as well as much of the first generation of the communist elite.

It was, therefore, only in the 1950s to 1980s that an established local communist elite, largely home-grown and home-educated, grew up. By the late Soviet period, this elite's solidarity was based rather on a shared interest in maintaining control over economic and social goods than on ideological commitment to the communist cause.

At the same time, the relaxation during the 1960s to 1980s of the Soviet regime's political, social and cultural control, coupled with growing disenchantment with the communist elite and its abuses of power, allowed the emergence of counter-elites, particularly in the academic and cultural arenas. It was these counter-elites who led the national independence movements and came to power in 1991–2, displacing the communists. They were, however, few in number and in most cases lacked administrative or managerial experience. Since independence new technocratic and business elites have also emerged.

Since 1991, at national and local levels in all three Caucasian countries, a complex and mostly obscure process has been in progress, as the old elite and the counter-elite compete, fragment, realign and sometimes fight over administrative and economic control. If this process currently defies detailed description, its main features are clear.

'Clans', 'mafias'[18] or patronage networks, grouped around powerful individuals and based on the exchange of favours and obligations, play an important role in the acquisition and redistribution of political power and economic goods. These networks may be based on kinship (President Heydar Aliyev's family being the most striking example), on professional or institutional affiliation (the interior ministry mafias, for instance) or on region (such as the Nakhichevan clan in Azerbaijan), but often they are not rooted in any social category, but fluid, coalescing around common interests and powerful individuals. The holder of any government position that gives control over economic resources (budget allocations, privatization, tax or customs receipts, regulatory responsibility for an industry, foreign aid or loans, etc.) or means of coercion (policing, border controls, 'protection', etc.) is in a position to become the centre of such a network. Clans frequently cut across ideological lines, with political or economic expediency making strange bedfellows.

In Armenia, for example while at national level the main political positions are occupied by members of the former nationalist counter-elite, many major enterprises are headed by former communists; at regional and local levels, however, much of the old Soviet elite has been able to hang on to its administrative and economic position, tailoring its ideology to suit the times.

In Armenia the profile of the mafia system is relatively clear, at least in outline. Until 1997, the most important networks were grouped around Vazgen Sarkisian (minister of defence), Vano Siradeghian (minister of the interior until late 1996, then mayor of Yerevan and subsequently ANM party leader), and Telman Ter-Petrosian (brother of the president and director of one of Armenia's largest enterprises).[19] Following the late 1996 cabinet shuffle and the resignation through illness of Prime Minister Armen Sarkissian in April 1997, two Karabagh Armenians took over top posts: Robert Kocharian became prime minister and Serge Sarkisian, already minister of national security, acquired the interior portfolio. The Karabagh mafia was already well established, distributing Karabagh's budget, including subventions from Armenia and diaspora Armenians, exercising general control over Karabagh's economy and handling the lucrative trade in contraband petroleum products from Azerbaijan for sale in Armenia. It now became a major player in Armenia itself, coming into conflict with established networks, such as that of Siradeghian. The death of Telman Ter-Petrosian in May 1997 also helped to clear the way for a realignment of networks within the country. President Levon Ter-Petrosian's waning support within the regime was presumably connected with this realignment and the increasing strength of the Karabagh Armenians.

Georgia and Azerbaijan present broadly similar profiles to Armenia, though in Azerbaijan the upper echelons are reputedly dominated by members of the Aliyev family, while other big players – Rasul Guliyev (former speaker of parliament) and Hasan Hasanov (former foreign minister), for instance – are progressively being squeezed out.

It can be argued that the emergence of such networks is in part a natural consequence of the absence of effective administrative, fiscal, financial and commercial systems: informal personal networks perform many of the redistributive functions that are carried out by the government and the commercial sector in developed political economies.[20] Moreover, the role of patronage networks, though not identical to those of today, was already well developed in the late Soviet period, performing functions that the creaking Soviet system left undone. What is undeniable is that the role of such networks has tended to perpetuate political domination over the economy in the post-Soviet period, leading to a peculiar form of transitional political economy.

Other factors have also contributed to this. The Soviet heritage of an economy whose visible parts, at least, were owned and directed by the state handed the new independent governments direct control over massive economic resources – all medium and large enterprises, for example. Allies and supporters were rewarded with appointments to key directoral and ministerial positions, or privileged access to information or the bidding process during privatization. (On the economy, see Chapter 5.)

That political patronage and protection are essential for business success is in part simply a continuation of the corrupt practices of the Soviet era, but in part it is also a characteristic of the counter-elites' relations with business from their time in opposition. In all three countries, financial support for the national independence movement, and more particularly for the paramilitary militias fighting for the national cause, came largely from voluntary or involuntary contributions from business. The militias' degeneration into mafia-style protection-racket activities was most blatant and prolonged in Georgia, but it was by no means unique to that country, nor to the militias of the early 1990s. The official security forces of the interior and defence ministries in all three countries are credibly accused of continuing the same activities to the present day.

Wars, blockades and political instability have further enhanced economic control by state agents. Interior ministries' functions in crime prevention and in guaranteeing the security and safety of persons, property and movement give them ample opportunities to reward or punish businesses and traders. Control of external borders gives frontier guards similar opportunities at a time when the rules governing the movement of persons or goods across borders are poorly established, or when circumventing blockades offers significant economic rewards.

Moreover, the links between Caucasian security forces and their Russian counterparts lend an international dimension to their 'mafia' activities.

Another factor contributing to state agents' control over the economy has been the channelling of new resources through state organs. All three Caucasian countries are recipients of significant sums in foreign loans and aid, so those branches of government that are able to establish a role in distributing these resources hold powerful economic levers. In Armenia this situation is of long standing, going back to the aid that flowed into the country following the catastrophic earthquake of December 1988. Control over earthquake relief aid became a bone of contention between the Soviet authorities and the opposition.

In Azerbaijan, as in other oil-based economies, the oil industry lends itself to state control through a state oil company and assorted government agencies. Control over this key economic resource has been a central objective of competing politicians, with an oil-related motive invariably invoked in any political unrest or important changes in the corridors of power. Huseinov's break with the APF government is often attributed partly to his frustration at being denied a share in lucrative oil contracts (the 1993 coup came just as the government was preparing to sign a major international contract). President Heydar Aliyev's son, Ilham, is vice-president of the state oil company (SOCAR). The resign-ation of parliamentary speaker Rasul Guliyev in 1996, ostensibly over policy differences, was widely believed to be a consequence of members of the Aliyev clan squeezing him out of a lucrative niche in the oil and gas business.

Transition to democracy?

The governments and all major political parties in Armenia, Azerbaijan and Georgia espouse the ideal of creating multi-party, constitutionally governed, secular democratic political systems. Since independence, all three countries have adopted at least one new constitution,[21] and have held presidential and parliamentary elections.[22] All have passed major political legislation, establishing, for example, the basis for the operation of political parties, of electoral systems and of the executive, legislature and judiciary. All have welcomed the participation of international observers at elections and have accepted assistance from international organizations, Western governments and NGOs in drafting legislation and developing practices to consolidate the process of democratization. Yet critics at home and abroad suggest that the commitment to democracy is no more than skin-deep, intended to placate the international community and secure Western aid and loans, rather than to make governments truly accountable to the people.

Constitutions

In the early independence period the 1978 Soviet constitution was maintained in all three countries, though its provisions were amended or subordinated to the acts of independence and other new legislation. The need for new constitutions was generally recognized, but drafting and introducing them has proved difficult.

In Georgia the Soviet constitution remained in force in 1990–92, though parliament made numerous amendments. In February 1992, following the coup against Gamsakhurdia, parliament restored the 1921 constitution of the independent Georgian Republic, abolishing the post of president in a reaction against Gamsakhurdia's dictatorial presidential style. Also in 1992, however, a new, directly elected office of chairman of parliament was created with Shevardnadze in mind, and subsequent to his election (with 96 per cent of the vote), a new Law on State Power was ratified, giving him an additional title, head of state. This in effect reintroduced presidential authority by the back door, but without fully clarifying the powers or division of responsibilities between the two offices occupied by Shevardnadze.

The inadequacies of the archaic 1921 constitution and the muddle of the 1992 constitutional arrangements, which were transparently based on *ad hominem* expedience (how to maximize the asset represented by Shevardnadze) rather than on political principle, gave urgency to the constitutional question in 1993–5. Debate focused on the pros and cons of re-establishing the office of president and of unitary or federal structures. In August 1995 parliament ratified a constitution that was very close to the draft proposed by Shevardnadze. It reinstituted the office of president, creating a strong executive authority on the US model, but with a sufficiently powerful and independent legislature (a two-chamber parliament, whose upper house will convene only after Georgia's territorial integrity is restored and the vague plans for the country's federalization have been implemented) and judiciary to provide effective checks. In spite of Shevardnadze's current domination of the political scene, the Georgian constitution does provide a basis for the consolidation of democratic institutions, and Shevardnadze has been obliged to take greater account of parliament and the courts than have his Armenian and Azerbaijani counterparts, though it is debatable how far that is a consequence of a better constitution and how far of the erosion of Georgia's executive power in the period 1991–5.[23]

In Armenia the period of preparation for a new constitution was less chaotic than in Georgia, but the debate over rival drafts even more acrimonious. From independence until 1995, the 1978 Soviet constitution remained in force, except where specific legislation superseded it, but as early as 1992 the ANM presented a draft constitution to parliament, while six opposition parties put forward an alternative draft in January 1994. The constitutional debate revolved around two main sets of issues. The first was the level of presidential power, which Ter-Petrosian and the ANM argued should be high to ensure strong leadership and stability in a period of crisis and transition. The opposition argued that the ANM draft would create a presidential dictatorship, with no effective separation of powers or system of checks and balances. The other major disagreement was over national issues, with the opposition pressing for easy qualification for citizenship and political participation for diaspora Armenians and for the inclusion of a clause on seeking international recognition of the 1915 Genocide.

In July 1995 the government-sponsored draft was adopted in a disputed referendum (official results showed 68 per cent in favour out of the 56 per cent of the electorate who voted), but it continues to attract criticism on the grounds of the exceptionally wide presidential powers it grants.[24] In 1998, following Ter-Petrosian's ouster, there was still talk of a new constitution and perhaps the creation of a parliamentary republic. Evidently wide constitutional powers were no help to the president when he lost the support of key members of his government and of the Republic bloc in parliament, while in the 1995–8 period the government's parliamentary majority was such that even a strong parliament would have been unlikely to offer any check on the president's powers. It could, however, be argued that the weak judiciary was an important factor in undermining the public and international credibility of the 1994–7 legal proceedings against the ARF and its members on terrorist and other criminal charges, and that more generally the shortcomings of the constitution contributed to the general political malaise in Armenia in the mid-1990s.

Until 1995 Azerbaijan retained the 1978 Soviet constitution, though precedence was given to the 1991 Act of Independence, and the Soviet constitution was revised in 1993. The weakness of Azerbaijan's parliament (the first independence-era election was held in 1995), the political turmoil of the early 1990s and the strict limits on political and public debate (the first draft of the new constitution was released to the public only on 15 October 1995, and the final version on 8 November – four days before the referendum[25]) prevented the constitutional issue from achieving the same profile as in the other two Caucasian states. According to official figures, the constitution was approved by 92 per cent of the 86 per cent of the electorate who participated in the referendum. As in Armenia and Georgia, Azerbaijan's 1995 constitution establishes a presidential republic, with the influence of Western models apparent.

In all three Caucasian states, the adoption of constitutions that clearly express the basis of statehood and of the political system, that stipulate the division of powers and that enshrine human and civil rights, is in itself a step towards democratic politics and a more accountable and law-governed society. Criticisms of aspects of the constitutions are well-grounded, especially those indicating the dangers of concentrating excessive powers in the hands of the president in the context of systems which in any case show a tendency towards authoritarianism and personalized politics. Yet perhaps more worrying than the failings of the provisions of the constitutions is their inconspicuousness in the political process. The Caucasian presidents' exercise of power appears almost unfettered by constitutional constraints. In all three republics, for example, incumbent presidents have taken advantage of crises to disqualify opponents from the political process with scant regard for constitutional niceties.

An optimistic analysis would suggest that it will take time for the principles articulated in constitutions to become established in the political culture; in Shevardnadze's words, 'the constitution will only have an irrevocable force when its ideas have put down roots in the people'.[26] A more sceptical view would suggest that there is little to suggest that the rooting process is under way (see below). The historical record supports the sceptic: while in 1990–91 both Armenia and Georgia achieved a change of government under the Soviet constitution, none of the several changes of Caucasian governments or presidents since independence have been constitutional.

Presidents

Presidents Levon Ter-Petrosian, Heydar Aliyev and Eduard Shevardnadze have dominated Caucasian politics in the 1990s. All succeeded in introducing constitutions that granted extensive presidential powers, but even before the new constitutions came into force their grip on national politics was well established. It was their ability, in the turbulent politics of the early 1990s, to assess configurations of forces, gauge the public mood, seize opportunities, forge alliances, dispose of rivals and build power bases and presidential apparatuses that placed and kept them at the pinnacle of national politics. In all three countries policy-making remains essentially a presidential prerogative, with ideas and other inputs coming from a close circle of senior ministers, advisers and aides around the presidents, rather than from government departments, parliament or wider public debate. The qualities they brought to the task tend to be characterized by supporters as statesmanship, strategic vision and determination, by opponents as authoritarianism, intrigue and ruthlessness; but setting aside the emotive evaluations, it is clear that each of them is a remarkable politician and national leader.

The level and character of presidential power are not, however, uniform across the three countries or over time. Ter-Petrosian always had the close support of a small group of senior ministers and advisers, several of them former Karabagh Committee members, who shared in power and had a say in decision-making. While it is early to judge, his successor Robert Kocharian is taking steps to open up the presidential system to a wider range of opinion and advice – by creating a Political Council, for example.[27] In Georgia, Gamsakhurdia took the personalization of presidential power to its furthest extreme, but Shevardnadze was obliged from the first to compromise with others, though he has succeeded in progressively dispensing with several of those whose support he once needed but who outlived their political usefulness: Kitovani, Ioseliani and Nadibaidze, among others. Nevertheless, there are other politicians of independent stature on whom Shevardnadze continues to rely, among them the leadership of the Citizens' Union of Georgia (CUG) party. In Azerbaijan, Aliyev's grip on power has developed along similar lines: immediately after he came to power in 1993, he was obliged to cooperate with others, but he has shed his erstwhile allies (Huseinov, Guliyev, Hasanov) one by one and now entirely dominates the political scene, with no minister or pro-government parliamentarian having a strong independent political profile or power base.

Presidential domination of the political scene has been facilitated by a political culture, perhaps most pronounced in Georgia, that admires strong leadership and is ready to accommodate its demands.[28] In addition, nostalgia for the strong leadership of the past – in reaction to the unfamiliar chaos of democracy and its failure to solve economic and social problems – has bolstered support for the 'safe hands' of the former republican communist party bosses, Aliyev, Shevardnadze and Karen

Demirchian, the unsuccessful challenger in the 1998 Armenian presidential election.

Levon Ter-Petrosian (born in Aleppo in 1945) was brought by his parents to Armenia in the late 1940s, when many diaspora Armenians immigrated, mainly from the Middle East. Educated in Armenia and Leningrad, Ter-Petrosian worked as an academic until the late 1980s, when he became a member of the Karabagh Committee. A stirring speaker at demonstrations, Ter-Petrosian personified the determination, seriousness and idealism of the national independence movement in Armenia.

His political talents were tested to the full in 1990–91, when he became speaker of the Armenian Supreme Soviet and immediately faced a series of crises which he skilfully negotiated, showing tactical flexibility in the pursuit of a long-term strategic vision of a strong independent Armenia, at peace with its neighbours, integrated with the world economy, but maintaining a special relationship with Russia. A pragmatist in office, his policies and leadership attracted strong criticism from opponents at home, notably over the implementation of radical economic reform, the attempt to normalize relations with Turkey, and the refusal to recognize the independence of Karabagh.

As president (elected October 1991), Ter-Petrosian was adept at balancing the powerful competing forces within the regime, but not at tackling the corruption and high-handedness of ministers. He never developed an independent power base, and his reliance on the 'power' ministries prevented him from controlling their excesses and ultimately proved his undoing. In the mid-1990s he increasingly lost touch with the public, appearing withdrawn and impatient of opposition and of the need to justify his position and policies to the electorate. He needlessly involved himself directly in the banning of the ARF in 1994, and realized far too late the extent of public disenchantment with the elections of 1995 and 1996. In late 1997 his conviction that Armenia's economic prospects depended on reaching an early settlement of the Karabagh conflict along the lines proposed by the OSCE proved that his political vision and understanding of national priorities remained clear, but the failure to engage earlier in the battle for hearts and minds, or to secure support among senior ministers and in parliament, marked the end of a run of successful escapes from tight political corners and he was forced to resign in February 1998.[29]

Heydar Aliyev (born in Nakhichevan in 1923) built his career in the Soviet secret service, becoming chairman of the Azerbaijani KGB in 1967 and first secretary of the Azerbaijani Communist Party two years later. He rose to all-Union prominence in the 1970s and 1980s, under Brezhnev becoming a candidate member of the Politburo, and under Andropov a full Politburo member and a first deputy chairman of the USSR Council of Ministers. In the Gorbachev period Aliyev endured several years in the political wilderness, but he re-emerged in the early 1990s as chairman of the Nakhichevan Republican Soviet, where he built up his original power base afresh, engaged in high-profile diplomacy with Iran and Turkey and bided his time until the 1993 coup against Elchibey.

His decisive action at that moment of opportunity left him, not Suret Huseinov, the principal winner. Since then Aliyev has shown his political mastery in consolidating his position and eliminating opponents and potential rivals. If he shows few scruples in disposing of possible political challengers, there can be no doubt that his political acumen is matched by a vision of a wealthy and independent Azerbaijan. At home Aliyev projects the image of a wise elder statesman with the experience to steer his young nation through the troubled waters of independence. When he returned to Baku in 1993, many expected him to revert to Soviet type and reorient his country towards Moscow, but he showed his grasp of prevailing national and international political and economic forces by taking over much of the ideology and policy agenda of the APF, not least the pro-Western foreign policy orientation and the use of oil as a tool in winning international support and underpinning Azerbaijan's independence. At the same time he has proved far more adept than Elchibey in managing relations with Russia and Iran. Aliyev's astute direction of policy also helped to narrow the gap between the government and the major opposition parties, leading to a less polarized and confrontational political atmosphere (at least until the presidential election campaign of autumn 1998).

Even opponents grudgingly recognize Aliyev's contribution to Azerbaijan's independence, though they do not forgive the price he has exacted in the suppression of political freedoms and in the corruption of which members of his family and his Nakhichevan *protégés* are reputed to be the major beneficiaries. Though in his mid-seventies and rumoured to have a heart condition, Aliyev shows no sign of slowing down and, following victory in the October 1998 election, has embarked on another five-year term in office.

Eduard Shevardnadze (born in 1928 in Guria, western Georgia), like Aliyev, was a member of the old Soviet elite and a candidate member of the Politburo under Brezhnev, but unlike him was closely involved in Gorbachev's reforms, when as foreign minister he played a key role in negotiating the Soviet withdrawal from Eastern Europe and the unification of Germany. Shevardnadze's fame and popularity in the West (as well as the loathing with which he is viewed by the Russian far right and left) stem from that time. Prior to that, he had been minister of the interior and then Communist Party first secretary in Georgia, showing exceptional zeal and initiative in tackling the problems of the late Soviet period. Opponents argue that the real Shevardnadze is the ruthless and scheming Soviet republican interior minister, but if he undoubtedly possesses those qualities, they are surely insufficient to explain his success or appeal.

Returning to Georgia in spring 1992 to lead the State Council, Shevardnadze is credited by domestic and international analysts with almost single-handedly turning Georgia around from the verge of anarchy to relative stability. Though he suffered several major defeats along the way, Shevardnadze has shown remarkable political talents, building a presidential apparatus before he became president and disposing of the other members of the State Council triumvirate, Kitovani and Ioseliani, both of whom led powerful military formations. He couples determination and personal courage with a sense of mission and a clear vision of Georgia's future, though he has been obliged to accept many unpalatable compromises in the short term. Far more than Ter-Petrosian or Aliyev, Shevardnadze appears a natural politician of the modern age, with a talent for the effective sound-bite (which he exploits in his weekly address to the nation). His popular appeal – at least relative to possible contenders – seems assured, in spite of the national humiliation in Abkhazia, the hardship suffered by most Georgians and the corruption and abuses that permeate his government.

In all three countries the current political stability was achieved under the leadership of a single president. This makes the issue of succession a crucial one in any discussion of medium- or long-term stability. Heydar Aliyev is over seventy-five years old and Eduard Shevardnadze seventy. Both remain vigorous, but age alone suggests that in both Azerbaijan and Georgia there will have to be a change of president within the next five to ten years.

Armenia has already achieved a stable, if forced, presidential succession. The country's longer experience of political stability, and the fact that, in spite of a top-heavy constitution, power was distributed among senior ministers rather than concentrated entirely in the president's hands has facilitated this. In particular the independent political standing of the former prime minister and current president, Robert Kocharian, helped to ensure stability and a smooth transition.

In Georgia the 1995 and 1998 assassination attempts on Shevardnadze provided a reminder of how greatly the country's stability depends on the person of the president. If Shevardnadze departs the political scene in the short term, before a resolution of the Abkhazian and Ossetian conflicts and of the tensions between Tbilisi and Achara, there must be strong doubts as to whether Georgia's political institutions will be able to effect a smooth transfer of power. The relatively open political atmosphere and developments in parliament and the party system point towards the potential for a viable democratic regime. Nor does Georgia lack potential future leaders – the speaker of parliament, Zurab Zhuania, is often talked of as a possible future president and there are other politicians of the younger generation establishing their credentials in parliament. These positive indications should not, however, conceal the underlying fragility of Georgia's political system or the extent to which it is held together by Shevardnadze's personal authority.[30]

In Azerbaijan prospects for a smooth succession appear more doubtful than in either Georgia or Armenia. The concentration of power in the hands of the president and the distribution of key political and economic positions to members of his family and fellow Nakhichevanis have created a regime in which there is a marked split between insiders and outsiders. Apart from the presidency, other political institutions remain weak, while Aliyev has not allowed potential successors to establish an independent standing in the regime. To date, presidential and parliamentary elections have done little to advance the democratic process and develop mechanisms for the smooth and legitimate transfer of power.

Aliyev has, however, pursued policies which have reduced the polarization between government and the nationalist opposition, and there is widespread recognition that prolonging the stability of recent years is a vital priority. It is, therefore, possible to envisage a post-Aliyev succession scenario in which members of the regime would agree to sink their difference and redistribute positions in order to maintain their hold on political and economic power, perhaps even seeking to coopt members of the opposition. It is also easy to imagine a scenario in which the ruling elite would fragment as today's outsiders moved to wrest key political and economic positions from Aliyev's protégés.

Elections

All three Caucasian states have devoted considerable legislative and administrative effort to the reform of their electoral systems. They have received support and advice from international organizations, Western

31

governments and NGOs on topics ranging from the drafting of electoral laws to the design of ballot papers and the training of election officials. These reforms have produced improvements in the way elections are run and have reduced, if not eliminated, a number of Soviet-era abuses. But to date, there is little to suggest that the reforms have achieved the critical mass needed to allow the ballot box to determine the outcome of elections.

This is an area where there is a marked divergence between the three states, with Georgia's parliamentary and presidential elections of autumn 1995 being judged generally free and fair by international observers (perhaps a generous judgment in view of the abuses that were observed – and the repression of Gamsakhurdia's supporters), while Azerbaijan's nearly simultaneous parliamentary election was condemned as neither free nor fair. The 1998 Azerbaijani presidential election was also considered flawed. Armenia falls somewhere in between, with observers returning an ambivalent 'free but not fair' verdict on the parliamentary election of July 1995, while the declared result of the September 1996 presidential election was judged unsafe in view of Ter-Petrosian's narrow margin of victory and the evidence of abuse in the counting of votes. International observers' reports on the two-round 1998 presidential election noted further improvements, but emphasized continuing abuses in the electoral process.[31]

Incumbent governments in the Caucasus enjoy significant advantages over the opposition in Caucasian elections:

- control of the electronic media, often coupled with denying opponents the stipulated access to the media during election campaigns.[32]
- exclusion of opponents from the electoral process, the starkest examples being the exclusion of the ARF from Armenia's parliamentary and presidential elections of 1995–6, of Azerbaijan's Musavat Party from the 1995 parliamentary election, and of Isa Gambar from the presidential election of 1993 – but these cases are only the most visible of a mass of disqualifications on the basis of alleged registration abuses or trumped-up criminal proceedings.
- disruption of opposition campaigning, sometimes through deployment of the police and security forces.
- intimidation of voters by the same agencies and local mafiosi at polling stations.
- vote-rigging, organized by interior ministry personnel, who have access to voter lists and know which voters have moved, emigrated or died.

- the abuse of state assets for electoral purposes: this covers a wide range of material and human assets, but perhaps most significant has been pressure on state employees – from soldiers, to teachers, to bus drivers – to vote for the government.
- preponderant participation of government supporters in electoral commissions at all levels, facilitating abuses in registration, balloting and the vote count: the under-representation of opposition parties on the Central Electoral Commission was the principal reason for the opposition boycott of the 1998 Azerbaijani presidential election. Isa Gambar (Musavat Party chairman) quoted Stalin's dictum: 'It's not who you vote for that matters, but who counts the votes'.[33]
- the survival among electoral officials and the public of Soviet-era attitudes to elections, which were viewed as occasions to celebrate support for the leadership and for friendly competition between precincts and regions to achieve the highest voter turn-out, rather than as opportunities to effect political change.

There has been progress in some of these areas – for example, opposition candidates' access to electronic media has improved in the period 1995–8 – and the sustainability of democratic reform is growing, with opposition political parties, NGOs and the independent media gradually developing their capacity to monitor the electoral process and challenge abuses. Moreover, in all three states elections do provide an opportunity for real political mobilization. Incumbents may enjoy significant advantages, but the outcome of elections cannot be taken for granted and active campaigning for public support is essential. In Georgia and Armenia at least, a mandate from the electorate does play a major part in legitimizing power, with Ter-Petrosian being characterized as a lame-duck president after his controversial re-election in 1996 and parliament playing an important, if not the leading, role in his ouster at the start of 1998. Nevertheless, the fact remains that the ballot box has yet to effect a change of government or president in an independent Caucasian state. By contrast there have been several changes of government by non-constitutional means. Measured by this traditional acid test of democracy, the Soviet institutions of the perestroika period performed better, with both Georgia and Armenia overturning communist regimes through elections in 1990–91.

Political parties

In Armenia, Azerbaijan and Georgia there is a range of political parties representing diverse ideological and policy platforms. In this sense the three countries have achieved one basic feature of pluralistic democratic politics. But Caucasian political parties are mostly weak and small, and do not play a central role in national political life. A number of factors contribute to this weakness. The three states are all presidential republics, and the constitutional strength of presidencies has been reinforced by the powerful political personas of Ter-Petrosian, Aliyev and Shevardnadze. Politics in general remains highly personalized, with a few high-profile individuals dominating the scene. In part this is a continuation of Soviet tradition where Communist Party first secretaries were the focus of regime loyalty, while prominent dissidents played a similar role for the opposition. The personalization of politics has gone furthest in Azerbaijan, where Aliyev supporters and the pro-government press form a sycophants' chorus to praise the president. Aliyev, however, has been careful to discourage the growth of a full-blown personality cult along Central Asian lines. In this context, the pro-government parties tend to become vehicles for mobilizing support for the president in parliament, while other parties often serve the same purpose for leading opposition politicians, readily splitting and realigning to keep up with the regular disputes and divisions that take place on a more or less personal level between their leaders. In Armenia and Azerbaijan in particular, the pro-government parties (the ANM and, since Robert Kocharian's election, the Yerkrapah in Armenia, and the New Azerbaijan Party) have poorly defined ideological or policy profiles, appearing merely as vehicles to mobilize government support in parliament and advance the careers of loyalists. The years 1997–8 saw significant party realignment in Armenia, with the ANM and several other parties and parliamentary blocs splitting and re-forming both before and after Ter-Petrosian's resignation; Armenia's party system remains in flux.

Few parties have succeeded in articulating clear and consistent policy programmes that mark them off from their rivals and could consolidate their support among particular social constituencies. Few have developed nationwide party organizations, large memberships or a sound financial basis (most depend on finance from business interests, exposing them to the suspicion of corruption and mafia connections). The absence of a visible presence or organization outside parliament means that they tend to resemble parliamentary factions more than established parties, a resemblance that is underlined by the complex and shifting parliamentary manoeuvres.[34]

There are exceptions to this pattern. Parties that are either direct successors to the old republican Communist Parties or inherited part of their assets, property, memberships and networks, or that are the successors to the nationalist independent movements which also developed extensive networks of supporters and local organizers, tend to be better organized and equipped (with offices, etc.), to have nationwide party organizations, and to have larger memberships. Among these are the Armenian Communist Party and the Armenian National Movement, the National Democratic Union (Armenia), the National Self-Determination Union (Armenia), the New Azerbaijan Party, the Azerbaijan Popular Front, the Musavat Party (Azerbaijan), the National Independence Party (Azerbaijan), the United Communist Party (Georgia), the Citizens' Union of Georgia and the All-Georgia Revival Union (Achara, Georgia).

In Armenia there are also a number of political parties that throughout the Soviet period had been active in the diaspora. These include the Democratic-Liberal Party or Ramkavars, the Social-Democrat Hnchak Party and the Armenian Revolutionary Federation (ARF) or Dashnaktsutiun Party. The latter in particular is well financed (from abroad) and well organized, having played a major role in mobilizing resources and volunteers for the Karabagh conflict. Between December 1994 and early 1998 the party was banned from political activity, though it was permitted to use its resources on behalf of other opposition candidates during election campaigns.

Parliaments

In a situation where executives are made strong both by constitution and through the leadership qualities of incumbent presidents, and where political parties are numerous, weak and bickering, it is not surprising to find that Caucasian parliaments have yet to emerge as effective political institutions. In Azerbaijan and Armenia, since the 1995 parliamentary elections, the huge majority of MPs support the government, which further vitiates the effectiveness of the legislature as a balance to the executive.

What survey data are available suggest that in the Caucasus, as elsewhere in the CIS, parliaments are unpopular, with the public having little knowledge of their function, and less confidence in sitting MPs' willingness or ability to fulfil a useful role in the political system. To some extent this may be viewed as part of a phase of disillusionment with democratic institutions and leaders and of the nostalgia for authoritarianism that are invariably sequels to the euphoria of attaining independence and democracy.

The Georgian parliament is a more effective institution than those in Armenia and Azerbaijan. The government party (the CUG) does not hold a majority and parliament has not invariably submitted to presidential will. It has, for example, on several occasions exercised its right to reject the president's ministerial nominations. Nevertheless, its strengths should not be exaggerated. It may appear impressive relative to Georgia's recent political chaos, and to the parliaments of its neighbours, but it remains very weak against the backdrop of Shevardnadze's domination of the national political scene.

On the positive side, there has been a growing professionalism in the way all three parliaments handle their legislative workload, though to some extent even this achievement has come at the expense of parliamentary debate. In Georgia and Armenia parliaments do provide an arena in which deputies can develop political standing and skills through debate and committee work.

Politics and society

Civil society

In the early 1990s, Western support for democracy-building in the Caucasian states was weighted towards developing political institutions and assisting with constitutional and legislative reform. More recently there has been a growing recognition that stable and sustainable democratic regimes cannot be achieved through the establishment of political institutions alone, giving rise to a shift in emphasis towards broad-based socio-political developments to underpin political structures. These developments are often discussed under the broad heading of civil society. Caucasian societies facing difficult political and economic circumstances do not provide favourable conditions for the spontaneous development of:

- a judicial system capable of defending the rights of citizens against arbitrary government action;
- independent, economically viable media;
- NGOs capable of lobbying on specific issues and mediating between government and society.

All three states have constitutions with provisions which explicitly protect human rights and provide for law-governed societies. These provisions, however, are not always respected or enforced. A serious weakness in all three states is the corruption and susceptibility to political influence of the judiciary. In Armenia and Azerbaijan the government controls key judicial appointments and there is no evidence that the court system is capable of bringing the government to book when it behaves unconstitutionally, or of protecting citizens' rights against arbitrary government action. In all three countries judges, like other poorly paid state employees, are generally viewed as thoroughly corrupt, with bribery playing an important role in securing a favourable verdict.

In all three countries human rights organizations have monitored numerous cases of arbitrary government action contravening citizens' rights. While there has been some progress – Georgia (1997) and Azerbaijan (1998) have both abolished the death penalty, for example – and a trend of gradual improvement may be discernible, the situation is still one of persistent abuse in certain areas that have long ago been identified and targeted by internal and external NGOs and other agencies. These areas are covered by specific constitutional guarantees and explicit government commitments. As discussed above, governments are still able to abuse citizens' political rights by manipulating elections. Opposition politicians have had their rights abused through arrest and imprisonment, violent disruption of political rallies and the arbitrary exclusion of individuals and parties from the political process. Incidents of arbitrary arrest, abuse of detainees (responsible for a number of deaths in custody) and abysmal prison conditions can be found in all three countries.[35]

The media in all three countries are unable to fulfil their role as an independent source of information, a forum for national debate and a channel for raising issues and expressing grievances. The constraints on the media have been significantly tighter in Azerbaijan than in Armenia and Georgia, though this may change following Baku's abolition of political censorship in August 1998. In all three countries television is now the most important medium for public information and the formation of public opinion. The only national television networks are state-owned and subject to political control over their programming (especially at crucial political moments, such as the run-up to national elections), though media monitoring suggests a gradual trend towards greater political balance and wider coverage. Independent regional television and radio stations are developing in all three countries and have broadened the availability of information and opinion. A number of these stations have encountered official obstruction of their activities, often carried out through the mechanism of the licensing system.

Newspapers covering a wide spectrum of political views are available in Armenia, Azerbaijan and Georgia, many of them affiliated to particular political parties. In Georgia and Armenia opposition papers regularly publish strong criticism of the government. In Azerbaijan they are more circumspect, but a range of opinion is, nevertheless, available. Most non-government publications, however, have very small circulations and are often confined to major cities. Newspapers without a wealthy proprietor face acute economic difficulties. This exposes them to government pressure, since newsprint, printing, distribution and often premises are available only through state-owned companies. The possibility of raising the price of newsprint, refusing to renew the lease on an office, or changing distribution arrangements gives the government strong leverage over many newspapers.

In all three countries certain subjects are off-limits to journalists, who generally exercise self-censorship to avoid the dangerous consequences of flouting the taboo. These include national security issues, excessively strong or personal attacks on the president (especially in Azerbaijan), and specific allegations about corruption and criminal business activities. A number of Azeri publications have been prosecuted or closed down for being too critical of the government, especially in the aftermath of the 1998 presidential election, while in Armenia all ARF-affiliated publications were forced to shut down in 1994 when the party was banned, reopening only in 1997–8. Journalists and editors have been pressured, harassed and occasionally beaten in the wake of reporting that ignored the unwritten rules.

Nevertheless, the gradual trend in all three countries is towards a broadening of media outlets, a greater balance in reporting by state media, and an easing of censorship and other constraints. Media legislation is being reformed, and for a privileged few there is growing access to international media via satellite television, and to electronic mail and other Internet sources.

In Armenia, Azerbaijan and Georgia alike, the independence period has seen the creation of numerous NGOs dedicated to a range of causes and issues spanning human rights, political reform, conflict resolution, media freedom, and humanitarian and environmental assistance. In rare cases NGOs have established national or even international standing and have been able to apply effective pressure on government. In societies with large numbers of well-educated and idealistic, yet under- or unemployed human resources, NGOs have provided a channel allowing a contribution from people whose energy, commitment and skills might otherwise remain unexploited. In this regard, even if they function partly as job creation schemes for the professional classes, they may fulfil a viable function. With few exceptions, however, NGOs are dependent on Western financial support, which can tend to integrate them more closely with Western and international agencies (for whose support they compete) than with their own societies or governments. The latter have shown resistance to opening up decision-making or redistributive functions to NGOs, while the wider society, with the exception of the direct beneficiaries of NGO projects, remains ill-informed about NGO activities and is not tied to them through the mechanisms of charitable donation and support. Those NGOs that have influence in the corridors of power often do so thanks to government or party political affiliation, which undermines their status and public image.

In short, while the growth of NGOs is an encouraging development in the region, they are neither sustainable on the resources of their countries, nor have they developed durable relations with state and social structures. This inevitably inhibits their ability to mediate between state and society.[36]

Legitimacy and ideology

A further serious political challenge facing the Caucasian states is the need to develop new legitimizing ideologies for governments that have now succeeded in establishing reasonably secure national independence and a measure of effective authority. Just as the nationalist counter-elite was obliged to adapt to a new role following independence, so the citizens of the Caucasian states have had to adapt their political role and participation to changed circumstances. For many of those who had sensed a personal role in shaping history through their participation in the mass demonstrations of the independence movements, this adjustment has proved difficult. Merely voting in occasional elections and referendums does not offer the same excitement or fulfilment as the direct action of the 1988–92 period.

People must adjust to a more nuanced politics in which they have to recognize that their governments are, if not necessarily the democratic choice of the people, at least more or less home-grown. They have long since realized that independence, far from creating the utopia that many had imagined, has by all social and economic indicators left them much worse off than before. Their leaders now are largely concerned with the mundane tasks of consolidating their own positions while attempting to run the state, manage the economy, develop stable relations with neighbours and the world and, most unpalatable for themselves and their citizens, reach compromise solutions with neighbours and minorities on precisely those issues about which their citizens campaigned so uncompromisingly before independence. Then it had seemed that independence would bring total victory for the national cause. Inevitably people feel that their hopes have been disappointed and that their governments have, to a greater or lesser extent, failed them and betrayed the ideals of independence.

Legitimacy, therefore, presents a potential problem for all the Caucasian governments. This might seem predictable for Georgia and Azerbaijan – where the nationalist counter-elites were overthrown in *coups d'état*, to be replaced by former communists – but in Armenia, where the nationalist counter-elite is still in power, the problem of regime legitimacy is no less acute.

To a great extent the problem is ideological. In all three states the governments now profess the political ideology of democracy, while recognizing that their regimes have some way to go before they become fully democratic. But the issue lies not merely in the imperfections of Caucasian democracy, but in the meaning and value attached to democracy by Caucasian citizens.[37] Even the Soviet regime always paid diligent lip-service to democracy; it organized elections and urged the electorate to vote for the party. The Soviet experience has done a great deal to shape public understanding of elections and party politics: the opportunity to vote in rigged multi-party elections does not signify an ideological watershed for people accustomed all their adult lives to voting in meaningless one-party elections.

Democracy was one of the demands of the national independence movements, but not so much in the sense of a constitutionally enshrined multi-party political system. The demand was rather for a national democracy, indicating the will of the people to unite and throw off Russian communist rule, restore and revitalize the nation, and defeat and crush its external and internal political and ethnic foes.

In the case of Georgia, Gamsakhurdia's continuing inflexible commitment to these ideals after coming to power was a major factor in his political downfall. Ideologically, however, he retained his credentials and is now seen as a martyr to the national cause by a group of die-hard disciples, the Zviadists. In Armenia, at the other end of the spectrum, Levon Ter-Petrosian proved far more politically adept, reaching compromises, adjusting goals and policies to political, military, economic and international realities, and striking deals with potential rivals, rather than relying solely on his supporters. But in so doing he sacrificed his ideological purity and relinquished a part of his legitimacy in the eyes of Armenian nationalists. From early in his presidency, Ter-Petrosian faced criticism on a number of fronts – economic mismanagement, corruption, authoritarianism, election-rigging – but none seriously shook his power base in the regime until autumn 1997, when he took the argument for a negotiated settlement of the Karabagh issue to the public and exposed himself to accusations of betraying the Armenian national cause. Only then did his support in government and in parliament crumble.

It would, however, be a mistake to conclude that in Georgia, Armenia and Azerbaijan the national cause is the prime test of legitimacy. The limited opinion poll evidence suggests that nationalist issues have gradually been losing ground to social and economic issues in popular priorities. The current weakness of regime legitimacy lies not so much in the current leaderships' inevitable failure to continue to legitimize their authority in the same terms as the pre-independence nationalist counter-elite, as in their failure to develop a new legitimizing contract with society. The Caucasian presidents all, to a great extent, base their claim to the right to rule on their ability to deliver political stability and economic progress. In the short term this may suffice to satisfy their electorates, especially in Georgia and Azerbaijan which have such recent experiences of political turmoil and economic hardship, but it may not provide a stable basis for a new regime: a cohesive political elite capable of sustaining itself through economic downturns, leadership successions and other crises thanks to public recognition of its right to rule.[38]

As long as the popular perception remains that clans and mafias linked to senior government figures play a more important role than democracy, merit or efficiency in determining political and economic success, as long as the new elites are perceived as essentially self-interested, and as long as the great majority of citizens live in difficult social and economic conditions while the elites enjoy conspicuous wealth, the problem of legitimacy will remain. The words of one voter, explaining her intention to vote for the government in a mid-1990s Caucasian election campaign, sum up this problem (as well as the malaise in state–society relations in the Caucasus): 'At least this lot are already full, but if we get others they will be hungry.'

Prospects for political stability

Compared with the early 1990s the South Caucasus has achieved a considerable degree of political stability. Cease-fires and protracted negotiations have replaced the armed conflicts that raged in Azerbaijan and Georgia between 1988 and 1994. Independence – the goal of the

41

national movements of the late Soviet period – has been achieved and does not currently appear to be exposed to serious internal or external threats. In all three states political regimes have succeeded in progressively (if still far from completely) extending their control over the means of coercive force. The degree of effective territorial control is less uniform. In Armenia the government is in full command of the entire territory of the republic. In Azerbaijan some 15 per cent of the republic's territory is in the hands of Armenian secessionists, but elsewhere government authority is well-established. In Georgia, both Abkhazia and South Ossetia are controlled by secessionists, while Achara and to a lesser extent Samtskhe-Javakheti are outside the effective reach of government.

All three states have adopted new constitutions and instituted major political reforms, though the depth of commitment to them remains uncertain and their implementation incomplete. Serious weaknesses in political development persist in all three states. Constitutions and political institutions remain weakly rooted, with presidential executives dominating the political arena and monopolizing decision-making. The legislature and judiciary have so far been unable to provide effective checks to executive power. This concentration of power in the presidency, and the weakness of other political institutions, are more pronounced in Azerbaijan than in either Georgia or Armenia.

Only Armenia has so far successfully achieved a peaceful transition from one president to his successor. In both Georgia and Azerbaijan there must be serious doubt as to whether the political system would be capable of negotiating a peaceful presidential succession, should the need arise in the near future.

In all three states the political economy is characterized by the dominance of patronage networks centred on senior government figures. Competition between these networks constitutes a parallel dynamic to the constitutional politics of political parties and elections. How far this intra-regime competition constitutes a threat to political development and cohesion remains uncertain.

In all three countries, while it is possible to talk about the development of civil society, that development is still at an early stage, concentrated in capital cities, and in important areas, such as human rights and NGOs, is heavily dependent on external assistance.

In none of the countries have new regimes succeeded in articulating effective legitimizing ideologies to replace the nationalist discourse of the late 1980s and early 1990s. In Georgia and Azerbaijan, Shevardnadze and Aliyev base their claim to rule on their proven capabilities in securing stability and promoting national interests and on the promise of future prosperity. In countries that have recently experienced violent political turmoil, these claims may carry considerable weight, but the forced resignation of Armenia's President Ter-Petrosian suggests that stability alone is not enough, particularly when the promised prosperity takes too long to arrive and other factors intervene.

For all three states political stability depends not only on domestic political developments. Shifts in international configurations, particularly any major change in Russian policy and behaviour, could still have a profound impact in the Caucasus. At the moment a combination of weakness and a pragmatic government in Moscow means that Russia poses less of a threat to the independence of the Caucasian states than in the first half of the 1990s, but the indefinite continuation of that situation cannot be taken for granted (see Chapter 4). In the medium to long term, political stability in all three states must be underpinned by delivery of the promised economic growth, an effective redistribution of material goods to secure rising living standards, better opportunities and some sense of equity for wider societies (see Chapter 5). Finally, the unresolved conflicts over Karabagh, South Ossetia and Abkhazia retain a strong potential to destabilize politics. Renewed hostilities and defeat would jeopardize the survival of any government, while the ouster of President Ter-Petrosian in early 1998 demonstrates that these issues are still readily able to occupy the political centre stage. These conflicts, and wider security issues, form the subject of the next chapter.

Chapter 3

Conflicts and security

Since before the collapse of the Soviet Union, the Caucasus region has been the location for a number of intractable and violent conflicts, which have jeopardized or complicated efforts to establish sovereign statehood, develop political institutions and civil society, and achieve economic and social reforms. This chapter will identify factors that explain the conflicts and insecurity that have affected the South Caucasus since the late 1980s, and consider the prospects for their continuity or change. The greater part of this chapter will focus on the three conflicts that have engendered wars, but it will begin by considering wider security issues and the emerging security policies of the three states.

Internal issues

Most Armenians, Azeris and Georgians (as well as Abkhaz and Ossetes) view security in terms of their nation's ability to defend itself from the threat posed by foreign enemies. This predisposition to see security primarily as a matter of self-defence against external aggression is in part responsible for Azeris' and Georgians' preference for portraying their republics' internal conflicts and instabilities as the work of external agents. It could, however, reasonably be argued that a view of security focusing on internal threats to individual and national security provides more productive conception of the Caucasian states' security situation. Many of the problems discussed in Chapter 2, as well as a number of issues in economic and energy development (discussed in Chapter 5), have a security dimension.

In all three states weaknesses in state-building and in the development of state–society relations leave citizens exposed to threats against their persons, property and political and human rights, both from unaccountable and uncontrolled state agents and from criminal elements (insofar as the two groups can be distinguished – for much of the last decade there has been a large area of overlap between them). Problems of nation-building, particularly the prevalence of narrow and exclusive criteria for inclusion in the national community, leave all those who 'fail' the test – ethnic and religious minorities prominent among them – exposed to threats emanating from the majority.

On this level of analysis, the outbreak of the conflicts over Karabagh, South Ossetia and Abkhazia can be understood in terms of the minority populations' concerns about the threats to their security posed by the constitutions and policies of the Soviet Union and the emerging new states of Azerbaijan and Georgia. What is certain is that these internal conflicts (see below), in impairing both territorial integrity and state sovereignty, have proved more dangerous to the national and state security of Azerbaijan and Georgia than any external threats.

Another potential internal threat emanates from other internal regional forces. Tbilisi has not only lost control over Abkhazia and South Ossetia, its hold over two other important southwestern regions – Achara (an autonomous republic bordering Turkey) and Samtskhe-Javakheti (bordering Turkey and Armenia) – is weak. The possibility of challenges from other regions too – Mingrelia (economically depressed, home to a high proportion of internally displaced persons (IDPs) from Abkhazia and to many Gamsakhurdia sympathizers) and Marneuli (with a large Azeri population), for example – cannot be excluded,[1] but the Achara and Javakheti issues require closer consideration.

Achara
Since the break-up of the Soviet Union, Achara, whose population is Georgian but mainly Muslim, has been ruled in more or less complete autonomy from Tbilisi by Aslan Abashidze. Through his All-Georgian Union for Revival Party (the second largest faction in the Georgian parliament) Abashidze also has a high profile in Georgia's national politics. There is bitter rivalry between him and the younger leaders of the CUG. Shevardnadze, however, has chosen to turn a blind eye to Abashidze's consolidation of Achara's independence from Tbilisi and has not challenged his more provocative expressions of insubordination, for example in rejecting the deployment of Georgian border troops (only

Achars would be recruited) and in introducing new laws on Achara's legislature, judiciary and security. The question of the extent of Achara's autonomy is so far being worked out ad hoc, on the basis of power politics rather than constitutional debate, with unpredictable consequences for Tbilisi's relations with other regions. Abashidze's position is strengthened by the economic benefits Achara derives from its position on the Turkish border and as home to one of Georgia's main ports (Batumi), but more importantly from the close relations he has cultivated with the local Russian military base, whose rank and file are mainly recruited from the local population.[2]

Javakheti

In this important respect the situation of Javakheti resembles that of Achara; here too there is a large Russian base (at Akhalkalaki), most of whose recruits come from the local population who also benefit from employment opportunities in providing services for the base. The region is poorly served with transport and communications to link it to the rest of the country and more than 90 per cent of its population is Armenian. The combination of these factors has tended to orient the region towards Armenia (and Karabagh – it is reported that Karabagh Armenians frequently visit Akhalkalaki to buy armaments), and a local Armenian organization, Javakh, has demanded autonomous status for the region. This aroused anxieties among some Georgians that Javakheti would become Georgia's 'Karabagh', but the diplomacy of Shevardnadze and Ter-Petrosian coupled with pragmatic and cautious Georgian policies on the ground – especially with regard to the Russian base – makes this a remote danger.[3]

Nakhichevan and Talysh

Azerbaijan also contains the potential for further conflicts between the centre and the regions, though Baku's strength relative to regional administrations is far greater than that of Tbilisi, and the absence of Russian military bases on Azerbaijani territory deprives potential rebels of one possible source of support.

Nakhichevan, an autonomous republic separated from the rest of Azerbaijan by Armenian territory, clearly has the potential to defy central authority (as it did when led by Heydar Aliyev during Abulfaz Elchibey's presidency). But the fact that both the last two presidents of Azerbaijan were Nakhichevanis seems to have led to an exodus of the region's ambitious politicians to Baku, and Nakhichevan has been docile since 1993.

In July 1993 an insurgent Talysh-Mugan republic briefly challenged Baku's authority. The Talysh are an Iranian people, whereas Azeris are Turks, so commentators perceived a new ethno-territorial conflict brewing. In fact, however, the insurgency was an expression of the factional conflicts in Baku (its leader was an associate of Suret Huseinov) rather than of a popular movement.

The Lezgin issue
There is, however, one regional issue which does have serious potential to destabilize Azerbaijan. The Lezgins are a Caucasian people numbering some 400,000 according to the 1989 census (their real numbers are probably considerably higher, as many Azerbaijani Lezgins are said to have concealed their true ethnic identity for fear of discrimination; Lezgin activists estimate their numbers at a million or more), and divided by the border between Azerbaijan and the Dagestan Autonomous Republic of the Russian Federation. Azerbaijan's Lezgins have complained of the denial of cultural and language rights and of economic deprivation. Their cultural situation certainly has compared unfavourably with that of the Lezgins in Dagestan. The post-Soviet establishment of an international border, which has been closed for a considerable part of the period from late 1994, has also been a source of concern, complicating inter-Lezgin relations, as well as causing economic problems.

A Lezgin organization, Sadval, has campaigned on Lezgin issues and some extremists have called for independence and armed struggle. Tensions with Baku became acute in 1993 with large-scale demonstrations and clashes with police. Moreover, there have been some signs of Russian interest, for example in the Duma, in exploiting the Lezgin issue to put pressure on Azerbaijan. Baku's response included the attempt to suppress Sadval, whose members have been convicted of terrorist offences. More recently, however, a more conciliatory policy has been adopted, involving cooperation with the Dagestani authorities and some effort to address Lezgin concerns, at least over the border problem. Since 1996, the likelihood of a renewed serious Lezgin threat to Azerbaijan's stability has receded.[4]

External threats and engagement in Caucasian security

All three Caucasian countries suffer from the security problems typical of small states: they are unable on the basis of their national resources to provide for their own defence (except perhaps in terms of threats

47

emanating from one another). The neighbouring powers (the Russian Federation, Turkey and Iran) – all of which are perceived as potential sources of threat by one or other of Armenia, Azerbaijan and Georgia – are far larger and stronger states which could easily overpower the defences of any or all of the Caucasian states.

Russia and the CIS

Russia's role in regional security is of special interest and importance. During the Soviet period the South Caucasus was part of the Soviet Union and fully integrated into its security system, with its share of army, navy and airforce bases, border guard contingents and early warning systems. In the late Soviet period Moscow had ultimate responsibility for dealing with the various conflicts that were already gathering force in the Caucasus. At that time, security matters were the responsibility of the Soviet ministries of defence and the interior, and of the command structures of the various military and security forces.

At the same time Moscow represented the entire Soviet communist system and Russian domination – the ultimate targets of the independence movements. Moscow was, therefore, attempting to fulfil the role of impartial arbiter and policeman, while simultaneously being a party to the conflicts. The incompatibility of these roles had become apparent long before 1991.

In the post-Soviet period Russia's role has become even more complex and opaque.[5] Even at the administrative departmental level, it has proved difficult to establish clear new guidelines for responsibility for formulating and implementing security policy in the region (see Chapter 4). The presidential apparatus, the Security Council, the ministries of foreign affairs, of defence and of the interior, as well as the general staff and local commanding officers, have all continued to play some role, but their policies and actions have yet to achieve coherence and consistency. Inertia has played a large role in deciding where Russia's military presence would be maintained. Commanders stationed in the several bases in Armenia and Georgia have enjoyed considerable leeway to develop their own local interests and relationships which have influenced security policy on the ground. The recruitment of local personnel into Russian military and border guard units has gradually eroded their 'Russian' character. The contingents stationed in the Caucasus could not readily be redeployed elsewhere – their local ties are too strong.

The original rationale for the maintenance of a strong Russian security presence in the South Caucasus was developed in the context of a strategy that hoped to make the CIS function as a security structure, maintaining the old external borders and strategic defences of the Soviet Union. This strategic intention is expressed by the 1992 Tashkent agreement on collective security, to which Azerbaijan and Georgia acceded in 1993, Armenia being one of the original signatories. The CIS, however, failed to evolve into an effective security system, leaving Moscow to attempt to pursue the same objectives in terms of Russian interests – securing its southern flank from instability and excluding foreign penetration of its sphere of influence – through bilateral arrangements.[6] This was the dominant feature of a far from consistent picture in the period 1993–5, which saw Russian debate insisting on great-power status and determined to exclude other external actors. Russia exploited Azerbaijan's and Georgia's conflicts and internal weaknesses to pressure them to fall into line on joint defence of the external borders of the former Soviet Union, the maintenance of Russian bases on their territory and the deployment of exclusively Russian (or CIS, which has amounted to the same thing in the South Caucasus) peace-keepers for the region's conflicts.

Resource constraints, the challenge of military reform (with its requirement for much smaller modern military forces), defeat in the Chechen war, and resistance from Georgia and Azerbaijan have led to an ongoing reappraisal of security commitments.[7] The 1997 Russian National Security Concept maintains the emphasis on the importance of the CIS states, but asserts that their development into 'friendly, independent, stable and democratic states' is of primary importance, rather than insisting on the need to corral them into a CIS security structure.[8] On the basis of this concept, it is hard to argue the case for the profile and distribution of Russia's current military presence in Georgia, for instance, even if one is prepared to accept the premise of Georgia's strategic importance for Russia. The commitments arose partly for historical reasons (bases were inherited from the Soviet period) and partly from deliberate policies undertaken in 1993, when Moscow required Shevardnadze to agree to demands for the stationing of bases and border guards in order to secure assistance in suppressing the Zviadist rebellion. At that time Moscow hoped that the military agreement would help to lock Georgia into an exclusive Russian sphere of influence.

Thus the question revolves not only around security interests and the resources to achieve them, but also around the question of the effectiveness of military strategies and levers to achieve broader Russian interests in the region.[9] Increasingly, Russian policy-makers and commentators have questioned the usefulness of the traditional zero-sum strategic perspective and the effectiveness of the use of military levers, but the debate has not been conclusively settled, and there are still voices calling for Russia to use military pressure – by supporting insurgents, for example – to force Baku and Tbilisi to comply with Moscow's demands.

Caucasian responses to Russia's military engagement in the region have been mixed. Independent Azerbaijan's first president, Ayaz Mutalibov (1991–2), relied entirely on Russian support in the military and security fields. Abulfaz Elchibey (1992–3) reversed this policy and vainly hoped for effective support from the West and Turkey. Heydar Aliyev has generally adopted a more conciliatory line towards Moscow, but has maintained Elchibey's inflexible rejection of the stationing of Russian troops or border guards on Azerbaijani territory (all Russian troops – with the exception of the personnel at the Gabala early warning base, whose status remains unclear – had left Azerbaijan by the end of 1993), and of the introduction of a Russian or CIS peace-keeping force for Karabagh. The perception of Russia among the Azeri elite and public is as a threat, rather than a potential ally and defender.

Gamsakhurdia (1990–92) resembled Elchibey in his rejection of a Russian military role in Georgia, but he was unable to achieve this objective, and Shevardnadze has accepted an extensive Russian military presence. Russian peace-keepers are deployed in both South Ossetia and Abkhazia, there are four Russian military bases (including one at Gudauta in Abkhazia) with some 9,000 servicemen,[10] and until 1998 Russian border guards were stationed at all Georgia's external borders. Only in late 1998 did Russia agree to a phased hand-over of all border guard functions, and Georgian units began to replace Russian in the same year. Shevardnadze appointed a pro-Russian defence minister (1994–8) and has sought cooperation with Russia in building up Georgia's armed forces. It is, however, open to question how far his acceptance of Russia's military presence and assistance has been voluntary.

Moreover, the Georgian parliament has refused to ratify the military agreement with Russia until the peace-keeping force (PKF) in Abkhazia fulfils its role in securing the return of Georgian IDPs. Many Georgian politicians and commentators see Russia as a threat rather than an ally, attributing Georgia's defeats in its internal wars to Russian support for secessionists. They question the purpose of the Russian military presence in Georgia, arguing that it does not serve their country's security interests (since it faces no serious external threat), but strengthens the hand of secessionists and of insubordinate regions. The border guards, they claim, do nothing but obstruct and delay travellers and goods in transit. Shevardnadze too shows signs of frustration at Russia's military engagement in Georgia. He has made use of CIS summits to criticize Russia's peace-keeping operations and his new defence minister is known for Western rather than Russian connections.

Armenia presents a marked contrast, not merely acquiescing in Russia's continued military presence, but actively welcoming the presence of Russian bases and border guards. In May 1997 it ratified a treaty, initialled two years before, establishing 25-year basing rights and a close military alliance. Armenians' benign view is coloured by history – Christian Russia has several times rescued Armenia from threats from Muslim powers – and the country has had no experiences of Russian manipulation of internal conflicts, and has no common border with Russia, which helps to dispel any anxieties about a Russian threat to independence. Close military cooperation has helped Armenia to develop its own military capabilities (see below). As in Georgia, Armenians constitute a high proportion of the personnel of Russian units (45 per cent of the border guards, for example).

The West, Turkey and Iran

If Russia's military presence in the South Caucasus is uneven, opposed by most Azeris and Georgians, and increasingly subject to scrutiny in Moscow, that country remains by a large margin the strongest external power in the region. Other actors, however, are beginning to play a significant role.

The West was initially wary of taking on any major security role in the region, recognizing the limitations on its capabilities there, reluctant to antagonize Russia, and uncertain about its interests in the region and whether they could be served by security engagement. That reluctance has gradually eroded as the need and the opportunities for engagement have presented themselves, and as Western states have developed clearer and more substantial interests in the region. Western and international organizations have acted as mediators and observers of peace-keeping in the Caucasian conflicts (see below). That role at first aroused suspicion and jealousy in Russia, but now seems firmly established, the UN and the OSCE being the principal organizations involved.[11] Western NGOs have also participated in efforts to promote conflict resolution and to build confidence.

In addition, the NATO Partnership for Peace (PfP) programme has provided the framework for Caucasian participation in a number of military exercises and training initiatives. Georgia and to some extent Azerbaijan are using the programme and the openings to Western military establishments to attempt to reorient or at least diversify their security relations away from dependence on Russia. The United States has engaged in some limited bilateral military cooperation with Georgia and to a lesser extent with Azerbaijan. Other Western countries have also made contributions in terms of training and equipment (for example, the United States and Germany have provided naval patrol vessels for Georgia). It has become common for specialists to talk of the Caucasus as representing the southeastern edge of the European security system, a conception which, if it takes root, will encourage further European and Western interest and engagement in the region's security. A number of Western states are committed to participation in an OSCE PKF for Karabagh, if and when the time for its deployment finally arrives.

It would, however, be a mistake to see Western engagement as rapidly developing to displace Russia, even if that outcome would be welcomed by many in Azerbaijan and Georgia. Even if the logistical capacity existed, Western countries would be reluctant to make serious commitments of resources or to risk the lives of service personnel in this remote region which means little to their electorates. Suggestions that NATO might take on a peace-keeping role in Georgia or establish bases in Azerbaijan have not been enthusiastically received in either Brussels or Washington.

All three Caucasian states are members of the OSCE and of NATO's PfP programme, though Armenia, anxious not to jeopardize its close military ties with Russia, has proceeded more cautiously than Azerbaijan and Georgia. The warming and clearer regulation of NATO–Russian relations were welcomed in both Armenia and Georgia as facilitating their participation in PfP.

Other external players are relatively marginal. Turkey's security relations have been mediated partly through NATO, but it has also developed bilateral security relations with Georgia and particularly Azerbaijan (a military cooperation treaty was signed in 1997). Armenia, however, views Turkey as a threat, a perception which is not entirely anachronistic, since Turkey is not only sympathetic to Azerbaijan over the Karabagh conflict, but as a guarantor of Nakhichevan's status (according to the 1921 Soviet–Turkish Treaty) has a potential pretext for intervention. Ankara hinted that it might feel obliged to become militarily engaged in 1992 and 1993, when there was fighting along the Armenian–Nakhichevani border, and following the massacre of Azeri civilians in Khojali, and has accused Armenia of harbouring Kurdish terrorists.[12] On several occasions there have been limited exchanges of fire along the Armenian–Turkish frontier. In addition to its close Russian ties, Armenia has signed military cooperation agreements with Greece and Bulgaria, two other countries with similar perceptions of a Turkish threat.

Iran, though bordering Azerbaijan, Armenia and Nakhichevan, has not developed a significant security profile in the region. Like others, Tehran attempted to mediate in the Karabagh conflict, but its efforts were upstaged by Russia. Iran has run camps on Azerbaijani territory for Azeri IDPs and, both at the end of the Soviet period when there were mass violations of the Azerbaijan–Iranian frontier, and when fighting in the Karabagh war approached its borders, has expressed serious concern at the threat to its security. Not a member of the OSCE, Iran is excluded from that organization's engagement in the region as well, of course, as from NATO initiatives. While neither Armenia nor Georgia feels threatened by Iran, many Azeris view Iran as a former imperial overlord and as hostile to Azerbaijani independence, and have accused Iran of supplying arms and other military assistance to Armenia and Karabagh.

The development of security policies and military forces

The governments of Armenia, Azerbaijan and Georgia have faced exceptionally difficult circumstances in attempting to initiate and develop national security strategies, military forces and doctrines. All have had to develop their armies and other forces from scratch, on the basis of paramilitaries and personnel recruited from the old Soviet army.[13]

Security policies
As small and weak states, Armenia, Azerbaijan and Georgia have had to develop security policies based on alliances with more powerful regional and extra-regional states, rather than relying primarily on their own resources. For Georgia and Azerbaijan this has presented special difficulties, as the dominant foreign military power, Russia, is viewed by many as a major threat rather than as a potential ally. There is still no other external alliance or set of external alliances that can counterbalance Russia's military weight in the region.

Internal challenges and conflicts have also complicated the task. If one of the functions of the military is to combat secessionist minorities, the recruitment of minorities into the military is called into question, but then the long-term consequence is to alienate minorities further and oblige them to look elsewhere for the means to achieve their security.

In the early independence period the nationalist governments of Gamsakhurdia[14] and Elchibey adopted military security policies that were unrealistic in terms of both the resources available to implement them and the regional balance of power. Without the asset of effective or loyal armies and interior forces, they adopted a tough line with secessionists and attempted to back it up militarily. Simultaneously, they challenged Russia's military presence in their countries and its regional dominance, but without being able to develop effective alternative alliances. The failure of these policies was responsible, at least in part, for defeat in the wars over Karabagh, South Ossetia and Abkhazia. Elchibey did, however, achieve the withdrawal of the Russian military presence from Azerbaijan, which has allowed the subsequent government in Baku greater freedom in developing its military and security policies.

Since 1993 Aliyev and Shevardnadze have adopted more flexible and pragmatic policies, abandoning the attempt to enforce military solutions on internal conflicts and adopting a more cooperative stance towards Moscow. At the same time they have sought gradually to erode Russia's dominance by diversifying their security relations, particularly through engagement with international and Western security organizations, with the United States and Turkey, and with each other and other CIS countries interested in checking Russian ambitions. The GUAM grouping of CIS states (see Chapter 4) has a security dimension, and Georgia has established bilateral security relations with Uzbekistan, for example.

Yerevan's security policies have been more consistent and more successful, being based on a more realistic appraisal of Armenia's own resources and its dependence on Russia. As noted above, Armenia also is diversifying its security relations, but continues to privilege the Russian connection.

Military forces

All three Caucasian states have faced the challenge of building national armed forces from scratch with limited financial resources and in conditions of ongoing war. The 1990 Conventional Forces in Europe (CFE) Treaty has provided a theoretical ceiling for equipment levels (the Soviet Union's quotas were divided among the post-Soviet states at the end of 1991), but in fact has been more important as an element in negotiations with Russia, which has been keen to 'trade' military assistance and equipment for a share of the Caucasian countries' CFE quotas.

Both Armenia and Georgia have entered agreements of this kind, while Azerbaijan has not.

In any case, the unregulated and ad hoc nature of the transfer of Soviet to national and paramilitary arsenals in the late Soviet and early post-Soviet period, and the continuation of unofficial arms transfers (most notably the clandestine transfers to Armenia of over US$1 billion worth of equipment, including heavy armour and tactical missiles, mean that theoretical or declared levels give only a partial picture of real levels, which may contravene CFE quotas.

Armenia's development of military and security forces began even before independence, in summer 1990 with the suppression of the Armenian National Army and other militias, and has progressed more smoothly than in Azerbaijan and Georgia. The close military cooperation with Russia has been an important factor – the quid pro quo for Armenia's acceptance and partial financing of Russian bases and border guards being free training in Russia for Armenian officers – but so has Yerevan's clear prioritization of military development, with budget allocations and other favours given to the 'power' ministries of defence and the interior, as well as the relatively high profile of Armenians in the Soviet armed forces, which provided a pool of officers and personnel for the nascent Armenian army.

The Armenian army has developed in the image of the Soviet-Russian model, the Yerevan-based ex-Soviet 7th Army, disbanded in 1992, providing its core.[15] Its armed forces are estimated at 53,400, with interior ministry troops accounting for a further 1,000.[16] While it is generally reckoned to be the most effective of the Caucasian armies, it shows many of the same weaknesses as the Azerbaijani and Georgian forces, if not to quite the same extent. From the outset the government has clearly articulated the principle of civilian control. A conscripted army, it has the weaknesses of the conscription system (corruptibility and arbitrary enforcement) which have a direct impact on morale and on the army's public image and legitimacy. Even since the 1994 cease-fire in the Karabagh war, it has proved difficult to secure sufficient conscripts for the army. In 1997 defence ministry proposals to end student exemptions on military service sparked a political crisis. In barracks conditions remain brutal and squalid, and have occasioned protest from the families of conscripts.[17]

Azerbaijan's military development began later than Armenia's and faced greater obstacles. The absence of cooperation with Russia, the lack of a martial tradition in Soviet times (Azeris, like other Muslim peoples, were virtually excluded from the Soviet officer corps), the politicization of the military around the time of the 1993 *coup d'état* and subsequently (for a time there were two defence ministers, one loyal to Suret Huseinov and one to Heydar Aliyev), and the mid-1990s succession of mutinies and attempted coups, followed by purges, all retarded military development. Mercenaries, including Afghan *mojaheddin*, fought for Azerbaijan in the Karabagh war, adding to the problems of lack of coordination and unified command.

Until 1994 Azerbaijan's defence depended mainly on units owing primary loyalty to their commanders, but since then the armed forces have developed significantly, showing markedly less reliance on Russia than the Armenian and Georgian forces. The army is estimated at around 70,000 strong, with 2,000 interior troops. The air force is considerably larger than that of Armenia or Georgia and it has a number of small naval vessels on the Caspian.[18] Nevertheless, most foreign experts still do not rate the Azerbaijani army's military effectiveness very high.

Georgia's regular army began to be seriously developed only in 1994, with paramilitaries having played the major role until then. As late as November of that year, Defence Minister Nadibaidze presented a frank and negative assessment of the state of the Georgian army. In contrast to the Armenians, there were relatively few Georgians in the Soviet officer corps. Since then development has been relatively rapid, with Russian assistance and models playing a major role, though there has been cooperation also with the United States, Germany and Turkey. The army is reckoned at over 40,000 strong,[19] though its combat readiness is open to question, and the problems of conscription and service conditions remain serious. Georgia has laid claim to a part of the former Soviet Black Sea fleet, though in fact its coastal patrol needs are being met with Western assistance.

Finally, the military forces of the secessionist republics are an important element in the regional security equation. Karabagh's forces are reckoned to be 20–25,000 strong, though this figure seems improbably high, even including troops 'on loan' from Armenia.[20] Abkhazia's forces number perhaps 5,000, but with a larger pool of reservists, and South Ossetia's some 2,000.[21] All the secessionist forces have combat experience, and victories have boosted morale.

The North Caucasus

In security terms, the North and South Caucasus are sufficiently closely interrelated to be considered part of a single security complex.[22] Direct overspill between North and South Caucasus conflicts has been limited, although Caucasian volunteers, mobilized through the Confederation of Peoples of the Caucasus, gave significant backing to the Abkhaz forces in 1992–3, and there were a few Abkhaz, Georgian and Azeri volunteers fighting against the Russians in the Chechen war.[23] The most significant interrelation between North and South Caucasus, however, rests in the context of Russian security policy – in particular the reassessment of capabilities and policies in the light of defeat in Chechenia, the waning of Russian interest in supporting south Caucasian secessionists, and the increasing attention to securing the southern borders of the Russian Federation (rather than of the former Soviet Union), with the borders with Abkhazia and Azerbaijan being closed for lengthy periods from 1994 onwards.[24] These trends have a strong impact also on the economic and energy security concerns of the republics to north and south, since all depend heavily on road, rail, pipeline and communications links across the border.

The distribution of the Lezgins and Ossetes across the border between the North and South Caucasus, as well as the broader sense of kinship between other Caucasian peoples separated by the southern border of the Russian Federation, tend to bind the whole of the Caucasus region together. Moreover, there is a clear consciousness of the interrelatedness of the North and South Caucasus, which means that developments, particularly constitutional settlements arrived at in any one of the region's conflicts – Chechenia, Ossetia-Ingushetia, South Ossetia, Abkhazia, Karabagh – will be seen as a precedent and will have ramifications for other conflicts and their potential settlement.

At the same time, however, the identification of a single Caucasian security complex should not conceal the fundamental difference between the situation of the North Caucasus republics of the Russian Federation and the independent states of Armenia, Azerbaijan and Georgia, which have far greater potential to diversify their security relations and eventually move out of Russia's orbit. Similarly, the scope for the involvement of external actors other than Russia is incomparably greater in the South than in the North Caucasus. Historically Armenia, Azerbaijan and Georgia have generally been more closely integrated with the countries to the south, east and west than with Russia to the north. The same cannot be said of the North Caucasus. So, if the Caucasus forms a single security complex, it is a far from homogeneous one, whose northern and southern constituents have markedly different potentials to develop security policies and relations.

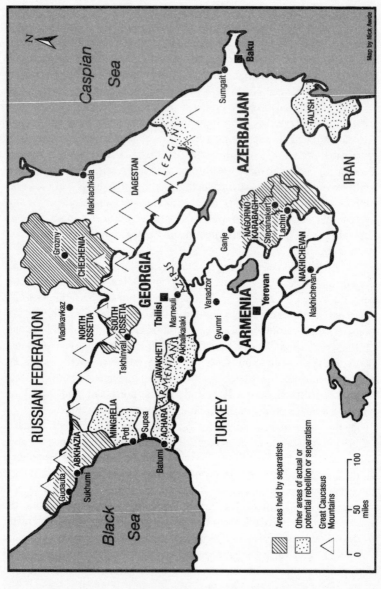

Map 2: Caucasian conflicts

Conflicts

The conflicts over Mountainous Karabagh, South Ossetia and Abkhazia have occupied a central place in the national lives of the Caucasian states. The late Soviet national independence movements crystallized around them and they have continued to shape political developments and remain a crucial factor in determining the stability or instability of the three Caucasian states. Losing wars against secessionists contributed strongly to the political turmoil in Georgia and Azerbaijan in the early 1990s, while differences within the regime over Karabagh policy brought down Armenia's long-serving President Levon Ter-Petrosian in early 1998. The conflicts have also been the focus of international interest in the region, and have had a profound social and economic impact, displacing hundreds of thousands of people from their homes, closing crucial road, rail and pipeline arteries, and greatly increasing the political risk of investment in the South Caucasus.

The lasting cease-fires signed for South Ossetia in 1992, for Abkhazia in 1993 and for Karabagh in 1994 have allowed the conflicts to move slightly from centre stage, but the fragile state of 'no peace, no war' in which all remain continues to impact on prospects for political and economic stability in the region and colours foreign perceptions of the Caucasus as a second Balkans, torn by complex and intractable enmities. It also leaves them firmly at the centre of the security concerns and policies of the governments of Armenia, Azerbaijan and Georgia.

The following sections will offer an analysis of the factors underlying the region's conflicts and the negotiations for their settlement, before proceeding to consider their similarities and differences case by case.

History and ideology

All three conflicts have been deeply influenced by the historical vision of the parties (see also Chapter 2). In each case the build-up to open conflict was shaped by a pattern of escalating claim and counter-claim, as the majority and minority nationalities contended for the exclusive right to the disputed territory. The strength of attachment to these claims reflects the specific Caucasian Soviet culture, in which both official and dissident thinkers gave history a privileged place in validating contemporary political and territorial claims.[25] The coexistence of contradictory historical claims was facilitated by selective use of sources, by tendentious interpretations and, on occasion, by deliberate falsification of the historical record.[26] It was further facilitated by the relative insularity of the republics' official and dissident cultures, which were able to construct and reproduce historical myths without exposing them to external debate or criticism. These myths gained wide public acceptance and inform not only territorial claims but also ethnic stereotypes: for instance, Armenians' view of Azeris as bloodthirsty Turks congenitally prone to genocidal attacks on Armenians and harbouring a secret agenda for a pan-Turkic empire; Azeris's view of Armenians as insatiable and aggressive irredentists, any concessions to whom will serve only to whet their appetite for their dream of a restored Greater Armenia. In the case of each of the conflicts the secessionists' self-perception is of an indigenous people threatened with assimilation, discrimination and genocide in its homeland. The Georgians and Azeris portray them rather as ungrateful late-coming guests, who have abused the hospitality shown them by their hosts and are now serving external neo-imperialist agendas in trying to dismember the Georgian and Azerbaijani motherlands.

These historically rooted myths contribute strongly to inter-ethnic enmity and competition for territory. Achieving the peaceful coexistence of the Caucasian peoples within multi-ethnic societies and state systems will call for major cultural adjustments, which inevitably will be slow to take root and will require inter-ethnic dialogue on many levels, as well as government promotion of a more inclusive vision of Caucasian statehood and society through deliberate educational and cultural policies. So far there has been little progress in this direction. Secessionist minorities' anxieties about the latent hostility of the majority national cultures is a significant impediment to their voluntary acceptance of inclusion within Georgian and Azerbaijani state, social and cultural institutions.

Constitutional status

In all three disputes unilateral declarations on the status of the former Soviet autonomies played a major role in the escalation of the conflicts, with secessionist and national governments soon arriving at maximalist positions. Abkhaz, Ossetes and Karabagh Armenians all believe that their lands were not historically part of Georgia or Azerbaijan, but were appended to them in the Soviet period for sinister motives by Stalin and his henchmen. They therefore seek to restore what they see as their historical status of independence or union with co-ethnics on the other side of artificial Soviet borders.

There can be little doubt, however, that the Soviet autonomous status was crucial in providing the secessionists with the political vehicles, territorial objectives and ideological articulation to pursue their independence struggles – in contrast to those minority peoples who were not accorded autonomous status.

Georgians and Azeris also see the Soviet creation of the autonomies as a sinister scheme, but they view them rather as artificial creations imposed on historical Georgian and Azerbaijani territories to facilitate rule from Moscow. They therefore have sought to reduce or annul their autonomy.

These two ambitions collided in the late Soviet period, when Georgian and Azeri nationalists tried to establish unitary nation-states, while Armenian, Ossete and Abkhaz nationalists sought to exploit the same legal and political processes to bid for separation and independence. The former succeeded in gaining Russian and international recognition, but could not secure control of the disputed territories. The latter succeeded in establishing independence, but have so far failed to persuade the international community of their constitutional claims. While they have gradually come to realize that international recognition of their 'independent republics' will not be forthcoming, they remain convinced that the constitutional processes by which they achieved independence were legitimate.

The constitutional dispute boils down to a secessionist emphasis on the principle of self-determination, and a Georgian and Azerbaijani insistence on the principle of territorial integrity. While both principles are firmly enshrined in international law and treaties, their interrelationship and appropriate criteria and forums for resolving their frequent clashes in real political situations remain elusive to consistent theoretical or practical solution.[27] The relative clarity of the notion of territorial integrity and its obvious importance for the maintenance of international stability contrast with the vagueness of self-determination. (What does it actually mean? The right to full statehood and sovereignty or to some more limited form of self-government? And who enjoys it? Does a small national minority constitute a 'people' entitled to this right?) In practice most states and international organizations tend to prioritize territorial integrity – the Final Act of the 1975 Helsinki Conference, for instance, explicitly constrains respect for the right to self-determination with conformity with international principles and norms relating to territorial integrity.[28] The inconsistency in the way these principles are understood and applied by the international community has engendered confusion and cynicism towards international mediation among the parties to the conflicts. While Baku and Tbilisi have counted on the international community's continuing prioritization of territorial integrity over self-determination in the Caucasian conflicts, the secessionists have seen this not as an expression of a principled, or even consistent, response from a post-colonial international system comprising nation-states and therefore inclined to tilt towards state interests, but as a result of specific international and Western economic and strategic interests (to secure access to Azerbaijan's oil via Georgia, and to bolster Georgia and Azerbaijan as a check on a possible future resurgence of Russian power), or simply because Shevardnadze and Aliyev have been successful in cultivating powerful friends in international political circles.

As regards future status, a simple return to the Soviet model of autonomy is impossible because it presumes the existence of an over-arching all-Union level of government, which was the ultimate guarantor of the autonomies' status. Nevertheless, it remains the model that is best understood in the region and that colours perceptions of alternatives. In the Soviet Union the autonomy of the autonomous republics and regions was as much a fiction as the sovereignty of the Union Republics. The Soviet experience has not facilitated contemporary solutions, since constitutions themselves and the concept of autonomy have been devalued. Moreover, public and political debate over possible constitutional solutions is characterized by oversimplification – reducing the issue to one of self-determination versus territorial integrity with no acknowledgment that there might be some middle ground where the two can coexist – and by ignorance of the wide range of constitutional arrangements that global experience is able to suggest.

Ter-Petrosian complained in autumn 1997 that there were only six people in Armenia who really understood the issues at stake in the Karabagh negotiations. He may well have been right, but if debate is ill-informed at least part of the blame rests with leaders who have been wary of going public for fear of stirring up opposition and constraining their scope to pose as nationalists at opportune moments. For as long as the detailed constitutional negotiations are carried on behind closed doors, while public debate remains ignorant and simplistic, there will inevitably be problems in gaining public acceptance of whatever constitutional arrangements may be agreed.

Even more than the details of the constitutional status, it is the problem of securing and guaranteeing any settlement that lies at the heart of the secessionists' reluctance to sign up to agreements. However bogus its constitutional guarantees, the Soviet system did provide some safeguards against excessive interference from Union Republican governments. This security may have stemmed from the centre's political interest in maintaining the autonomies as a check on Georgian and Azerbaijani national aspirations, but it was intermittently effective for all that.

The absence of any equivalent permanent external guarantor from the constitutional settlements tabled for the Caucasian conflicts is acutely felt by the secessionists. Their leaders in Stepanakert, Tskhinvali and Sukhumi do not trust Baku and Tbilisi to respect whatever agreement may be reached. Even if they could be persuaded of Aliyev's and Shevardnadze's good faith, they are aware that most other political forces in Azerbaijan and Georgia, as well as public opinion, are more hard-line than the ageing incumbent presidents. They also observe Azerbaijan's and Georgia's political instability and poor record of respect for constitutions and for the rights of even the majority nationality. Currently the secessionists fear that inclusion in an Azerbaijani or Georgian state structure will expose them to arbitrary and unaccountable government, and that once they have agreed a settlement, the international community will be only too glad to wash its hands of their fate, dismissing any future violations as the internal affairs of the state in question.

For the relatively long period that will be needed to establish trust, international guarantees will be required, perhaps even some permanent method of direct appeal to or representation at international level for the secessionists. Alternatively such guarantees could be provided by individual states (Armenia, Russia and Iran have been mooted for Karabagh, for instance), but while this would save the international community from open-ended commitments and costs, it might prove even more unpalatable for Baku and Tbilisi.

Military balance
At decisive moments during the conflict the secessionists, thanks largely to external support, enjoyed a significant military advantage over the Azerbaijani and Georgian forces. As indicated in an earlier section, the situation today is changing. While Karabagh can still rely on Armenian support, the Ossetes and Abkhaz may not be able to count on the backing from Russia and the North Caucasus that they received during the fighting in the early 1990s. Moreover, the Azerbaijani and Georgian armies, though still weak, are already more formidable than the odd assortment of forces they were able to field in the early 1990s. Thus the trend seems to be set for the balance to shift further away from the secessionists. It can be predicted that Azerbaijan's larger population and oil revenues will eventually give it an advantage over even the combined forces of Karabagh and Armenia.

Consciousness of the shift in the military balance is evident in all parties, though the secessionists may try to deny it and cherish the myth that their victories were won single-handed. The crucial question is how that consciousness will feed into decisions over settlement or renewed hostility. The Azeris and Georgians, and to some extent the international community, clearly expect or hope that it will lead to a sober reassessment of the long-term prospects of the secessionist republics and hence to a greater flexibility in negotiation. This outcome, however, is far from assured, and statements by some secessionists, for example the Karabagh defence minister Samvel Babayan, suggest an alternative response, namely that the secessionists might be tempted to launch a pre-emptive strike before their military advantage ebbs away. The precise military objectives of such a strike are open to speculation: for the Karabagh forces they might include attacking Azerbaijan's road, rail and pipeline links with Georgia, or the seizure of further territory. Such sentiments do not reflect formal positions, and for the moment it appears that the military balance is too even (or too difficult to assess) for any party seriously to consider resuming full-scale hostilities. They do, however, indicate that shifts in the military balance may elicit unpredictable responses. Military leverage on the secessionists is as likely to hamper as to facilitate a more conciliatory approach to negotiations.

Economic dimensions: blockades and incentives
All three conflicts caused great economic and material damage and wrecked the economies of the secessionist territories. Blockades of Abkhazia, Karabagh and Armenia have caused further economic damage. Those applying the blockades do so in the expectation that economic pressure will induce parties to make concessions at the negotiating table. Economic pressure appears to be the only lever Azerbaijan can apply to Armenia and the Karabagh Armenians.

Experience seems to suggest, however, that blockades, like sanctions, are not reliable policy tools for eliciting specific responses. In Karabagh and Abkhazia economic hardship seems only to have reinforced the siege mentality, at least among leaders (who do not suffer the same consequences of a blockade as the wider population). In Armenia the response has been more complex, with Ter-Petrosian openly arguing that the economic necessity of lifting the blockade made a resolution urgent (though he did not admit that it would lead to additional Armenian concessions). Even that, however, elicited a forceful denial in the media and from his opponents in the regime, who condemned the idea of making concessions on Karabagh merely to secure Armenia's economic well-being and accused Ter-Petrosian of selling out the Karabagh cause.

In short, in Armenia too, the response to blockade seems to have been a hardening rather than a softening of positions.

Another consequence of blockades is that they remove the possibility for human contact, and therefore for the confidence-building measures and gradual restoration of social relations and economic interdependence which are essential to erode this distrust and to allow new inter-ethnic relations to be established. It is precisely the absence of a blockade and the possibility of developing these areas that marks off the South Ossetian conflict from those in Karabagh and Abkhazia. In Karabagh and Abkhazia those confidence-building processes have not begun, and the chance of the secessionists accepting a settlement is correspondingly more remote.

Furthermore, blockades contribute to the problems of criminality, corruption and smuggling, providing those charged with enforcing embargoes and guarding borders (military, police and border guard forces) with economic opportunities and vested interests in prolonging the status quo. This applies on both sides of the blockaded borders.[29]

It is unlikely that Tbilisi or Baku will relinquish their policies of economic pressure, but it should be recognized that the blockades, while they are certainly hurting the Abkhaz and the Armenians, have not proved effective in pressuring them into a settlement, while they preclude the possibility of confidence-building measures.

Economic carrots as well as sticks may be applied to the conflicts. In South Ossetia international commitments to help rebuild infrastructure once a settlement is in place provide a clear incentive to the secessionists to negotiate a resolution, but without subjecting them to coercion. Azerbaijani hints that a pipeline might be built across Karabagh and Armenia if the conflict is resolved, however, have produced a mainly negative response from Armenians, who have characterized this as a 'bribe'. Armenian officials have consistently emphasized that there can be no linkage between pipelines and peace negotiations.

Karabagh

Development of the conflict
In February 1998 Armenia and Karabagh celebrated the tenth anniversary of the Karabagh movement, providing a reminder that this is the longest running of all post-Soviet disputes.[30] The conflict's roots go much further back – to the 1920s Soviet demarcation of republican borders and creation of the Mountainous Karabagh Autonomous Region (*oblast*), in a period when the Bolsheviks were seeking rapprochement

with Turkey and therefore tended to support Azerbaijani rather than Armenian claims; beyond that, its roots go back to the Armenian aspiration, expressed as early as the eighteenth century, to create an Armenian nation-state comprising the territories that had historical Armenian populations, even though for centuries they had been ruled by Muslim Iranians and Turks and had multi-ethnic populations. Incompatible Armenian and Azerbaijani claims to exclusive ethnic homelands provide the ideological dimension to the conflict.[31]

The immediate grievances of the Karabagh Armenians in 1988 were that their region was starved of resources by Baku, that they were denied proper cultural rights, and that Azerbaijan followed a deliberate policy of encouraging Azeri settlement in order to shift the demographic balance (Armenians had comprised 94 per cent of the population in 1921, but only 76 per cent in 1979), with the long-term objective of squeezing the Armenians out. Their initial demand was for transfer from Azerbaijani to Armenian jurisdiction. The Supreme Soviet of Armenia and the National Council of Karabagh in December 1989 declared the unification of Karabagh and Armenia. Subsequently, in view of the international difficulties this step would cause for Armenia, the demand was changed to one for independence. The Karabagh Armenians held a referendum in December 1991 and declared the independent Mountainous Karabagh Republic in January 1992. To date, the republic has not been recognized by any state, including Armenia. Azerbaijan's Supreme Soviet responded to the declaration of unification by dissolving the region and annulling its autonomy in August 1990 and October 1991.

The course of the conflict has been complex and has had direct ramifications far beyond Karabagh's borders. Some 200,000 Armenians fled their homes in Azerbaijan, mostly to Armenia and Karabagh, but some 45,000 to Russia. The 185,000 Azeris and 11,000 Muslim Kurds who lived in Armenia, as well as the 47,000 Karabagh Azeris, were compelled to emigrate to Azerbaijan. In addition, a further 500,000–600,000 Azeris have been forced from their homes in the districts of Agdam, Fizuli, Jebrail, Kelbajar, Kubatly, Lachin and Zangelan.[32]

From 1989 Azerbaijan has imposed a more or less continuous blockade of road, rail and energy links with Armenia, and Turkey has supported the blockade along its border with Armenia. Armenia has closed its borders with Nakhichevan. The blockade has caused severe economic difficulties for Armenia, notably an intense energy crisis in 1992–3. Hostilities have spread far beyond the borders of Karabagh, with episodes of fighting all along Armenia's borders with Azerbaijan and Nakhichevan. In recent years, cease-fire violations have occurred as frequently across the Armenian–Azerbaijani border as across the cease-fire line.

Between 1988 and 1994 the conflict followed a pattern of interrupted escalation against a background of continuous efforts to negotiate a cease-fire on the part of a range of mediators (including Russia, Turkey, Iran, Kazakhstan and various Western countries and international organizations). For most of 1989 Karabagh was under a special administration answerable directly to Moscow. For much of 1990 and 1991 the Soviet government sided with Baku, dispatching interior ministry forces to support Azerbaijani operations against Armenian villages in and around Karabagh. Since the collapse of the Soviet Union, however, Russia has supported the Armenian side, offering substantial military support to Armenia. The revelations in spring 1997 of some $1 billion worth of unofficial (and in contravention of the CFE treaty) Russian arms deliveries to Armenia, including tanks and long-range missiles (many of which are believed to be deployed in Armenian-held areas within Azerbaijan), merely confirmed the established pattern.

Armenia itself, while never formally at war with Azerbaijan and denying direct involvement, has contributed financially and materially to the Karabagh war effort. Convincing evidence points also to the direct engagement of Armenian armed forces in the fighting, and to their continued regular stationing in Karabagh. Turkey has lent support to Azerbaijan, but has lacked the direct access to allow large-scale supplies and, under pressure both from other NATO members and from Russia, has been circumspect in its assistance, which has mostly been restricted to military training and to maintaining diplomatic and economic pressure on Armenia.

Military advantage has swung between the two sides, with Azerbaijani forces besieging Stepanakert (Karabagh's capital) for much of 1991–2 and taking nearly half of Karabagh in the summer of 1992. Armenian forces had the upper hand in fighting in winter and spring 1992 (when Khojali, Shushi/Shusha and the Lachin corridor were taken), and in most of 1993 and early 1994 when Kelbajar and extensive territories outside Karabagh fell to Armenian forces. In December 1993 a major Azerbaijani offensive failed to achieve significant lasting territorial gains.

Negotiations and the status quo
In May 1994 the sides agreed to a cease-fire brokered by Russia, and in July of the same year Armenia, Azerbaijan and Karabagh all committed themselves to maintaining it and seeking a negotiated settlement. The

OSCE (formerly CSCE) is committed to providing a PKF once the sides have agreed on force separation and repatriation, but agreement has still not been reached, and the parties face each other at short range all along the cease-fire line. There are frequent minor violations of the cease-fire, but so far these have not been allowed to escalate. Presidents Aliyev and Ter-Petrosian used regularly to telephone each other to defuse potential crises.

The cease-fire left Armenian forces in control of almost 15 per cent of Azerbaijani territory, of which roughly one-third is accounted for by Karabagh itself. (Azerbaijani sources regularly claim that 20 per cent or more of their territory is occupied but independent specialists calculate the percentage to be considerably lower.[33]) Estimates of the casualties range from 15,000 to 25,000 killed. In addition to combatant and civilian casualties during military operations the conflict gave rise to several pogroms against Armenian civilians in Azerbaijan, the most notorious occurring in Sumgait in 1988 and in Baku in 1990. Azeri civilians were massacred following the Armenian capture of the village of Khojali in 1992. The eviction of the Armenian population of Azerbaijan and the Azeri population of Armenia was accompanied by serious human rights abuses. The informal nature of the conflict (the parties have never made a declaration of war) has led to a blurring of civilian and military lines and to numerous abuses in the treatment of prisoners and hostages.

The period 1994–8 has seen the status quo frozen, allowing the consolidation of Karabagh's *de facto* independence and the development of its links with Armenia. Efforts to achieve a resolution have been in progress since long before the 1994 cease-fire. Currently the two main mediators are Russia and the OSCE. It was Russia that eventually brokered the cease-fire and Moscow has maintained an active diplomacy with both Armenia and Azerbaijan. But Russia's ability to facilitate negotiations and eventual peace has been undermined by a number of factors. Moscow has been too deeply involved in the conflict from its outset to act as an impartial broker. Azerbaijan remains suspicious of Russian motives and long-term Russian objectives in the Caucasus and has rejected proposals for exclusively Russian or CIS peace-keeping. Russian policy has been inconsistent, with a number of discordant voices expressing contradictory Russian interests and policies.

The main international vehicle working for a resolution is the Minsk Group of member states the OSCE, which began conducting negotiations as early as January 1992.[34] The OSCE's efforts have been supported by the United Nations and the international community. But the organization's effectiveness for much of this period has been hampered by internal differences, by the low priority accorded to Karabagh by some members of the Minsk Group, and also by the reluctance of Western states to commit themselves to peace-keeping operations in the remote Caucasus. Most damaging was the deliberate undercutting of OSCE initiatives by Russia in 1993–4, a period when Moscow was determined to keep the Caucasus in its exclusive sphere of influence and still hoped to negotiate the deployment of a Russian or CIS force. The latter problem was partially overcome in December 1994 when the OSCE recognized Russia's special claims by making it a permanent co-chair of the Minsk Group, a move which succeeded in bringing Russian initiatives under the OSCE umbrella. In parallel to the international talks, Yerevan and Baku established a bilateral dialogue at presidential adviser level to try to push matters forward.

The years 1996–7 saw a noticeable increase in diplomatic activity and pressure with the new Russian foreign minister Yevgenii Primakov and the new US Secretary of State Madeleine Albright committing their governments to a more active role in the Caucasus. In 1997 the Minsk Group gained greater international weight when the United States and France joined Russia as co-chairs. In December 1996, on Azerbaijan's prompting, the OSCE summit in Lisbon sought to include a statement of principles for the resolution of the conflict. These included the preservation of Azerbaijan's territorial integrity, which Armenia rejected as predetermining the status of Karabagh. The summit, hailed as a diplomatic victory for Azerbaijan, revealed the extent of Armenia's and Karabagh's international isolation, but far from injecting a new spirit of realism into their position on the issue, this merely awakened old memories of international betrayal and confirmed the opinion of those who believe that Armenians have to be self-reliant rather than trusting an international community all too ready to succumb to the blandishments of Azerbaijan's oil diplomacy.

In 1997 the Minsk Group submitted successive proposals for a phased settlement. By autumn Baku and Yerevan were ready to accept these, at least as the basis for negotiation, but Stepanakert rejected them. These apparently encouraging developments at the international negotiating table took place, however, in parallel to a post-Lisbon summit atmosphere of mounting suspicion and intransigence in Armenia and Karabagh. When in September Ter-Petrosian publicly endorsed the Minsk Group proposals and attempted to pressure the Karabagh leadership to fall into line, the extent to which he had lost popularity and authority was revealed by an uproar of opposition and accusations that he was betraying Karabagh. This set in motion the train of events that forced his resignation in February 1998.

President Kocharian will doubtless avoid Ter-Petrosian's error in placing himself in a position where he could be accused of betraying Karabagh. Armenia's standard official line – that it will support any settlement acceptable to Karabagh, and that Baku should enter direct talks with Stepanakert – has been re-emphasized by the new government, which has also demanded a larger role for the Karabagh Armenians in the negotiations. Baku has always resisted direct negotiations with Stepanakert, arguing that they would lend legitimacy to the Karabagh leadership, that if Karabagh Armenians are represented, Karabagh Azeris also should be, and that in any case Karabagh is really Yerevan's instrument rather than an independent party. The last argument at least has been exposed as a myth by the 1997–8 political developments in Armenia; if Yerevan and Stepanakert are parts of the same animal, it is clearly the Karabagh tail that has been wagging the Armenian dog.

The main issues in contention between the parties are:

- the status of Karabagh: Stepanakert, while reaffirming Karabagh's independence, has hinted that this could be *de facto* rather than *de jure*. It rejects any vertical subordination to Baku and insists on real sovereignty. Baku has stated that it is ready to grant Karabagh the highest degree of autonomy, but without elaborating on what this entails. The constitution of Azerbaijan, which stipulates a unitary state, may require revision to accommodate any eventual settlement.
- Armenian withdrawal from Azerbaijani territory outside Karabagh: while in principle the Armenian side accepts the eventual return of most of these territories, in practice the Karabagh leadership refuses to relinquish them prematurely, seeing them as both a guarantee of Karabagh's security and its best bargaining chip. In some of these territories, notably Lachin, there has been Armenian settlement, while others contain Armenian historical and cultural monuments; this factor further complicates their return.
- Karabagh's security: Stepanakert insists on strong security guarantees in recompense for giving up the territories it now holds. In addition to the maintenance of Karabagh's own security forces, this would entail the long-term deployment of a PKF and international security guarantees against possible future Azerbaijani attack. Stepanakert also demands the permanent maintenance of the Lachin corridor to allow unrestricted communication with Armenia. The current Minsk Group

proposals are understood to include a complex leasing arrangement for Lachin which is unlikely to satisfy this demand.

- the return of refugees and control of Shushi/Shusha: Baku demands that Karabagh Azeris should be permitted to return to their homes with appropriate arrangements for their security. Stepanakert argues that if provision is made for the return of Karabagh Azeris, it should also be made for the hundreds of thousands of other refugees and displaced persons created by the conflict. The issue has special significance, as many of the Azeris would return to Shushi/Shusha, whose population was 90 per cent Azeri at the start of the conflict (though historically the town had a large Armenian population; it is of great symbolic and cultural significance to both sides). The town is situated on a strategic height overlooking Stepanakert, and it was principally from Shushi/Shusha that the Azeris bombarded Stepanakert for most of 1992. This stiffens the Karabagh Armenians' reluctance to relinquish it, even to international peace-keepers.

Difficult as these issues may be, the stumbling block for the 1997 Minsk Group proposals and the issue on which a serious divergence opened between Ter-Petrosian and the Karabagh leadership was the schedule for resolving the crisis. International mediators and the Armenian and Azerbaijani governments reached the conclusion that it would not be possible to resolve all the most difficult issues in one stage: it would be necessary first to resume economic and human links to allow trust and interdependence to build before tackling questions such as status. The Minsk Group therefore proposed a phased settlement, with a first stage when Armenians would withdraw from the territories outside Karabagh, refugees would return to their homes, the PKF would deploy and borders would reopen. In a second stage Karabagh's status would be decided, though it was clear that it would be essentially self-governing, while Azerbaijan's territorial integrity would be formally preserved. The Karabagh leadership, supported by Robert Kocharian and other senior government figures in Yerevan, was strongly opposed to the phased approach, objecting that Karabagh was required to give up territory at the first stage, while Azerbaijan might subsequently change its position on the status issue or renege on its agreements regarding any of the first-phase issues (e.g. the mandate and duration of the PKF, the arrangements for Lachin, etc.). Stepanakert argued instead for a 'package' solution that would resolve status and all major issues in a single settlement. Karabagh's rejection of a phased settlement is shared by Robert Kocharian's government.

Prospects

In assessing the prospects for a resolution it is necessary to focus more closely on the interests and incentives, strengths and weaknesses of the conflicting parties.

In Azerbaijan most opposition parties advocate a tougher stance than that of President Aliyev; some are convinced that time and oil revenue are so clearly on Azerbaijan's side that it is better to wait for the balance to shift in order to secure a more favourable outcome or, if necessary, exercise the military option. But there is little doubt that Aliyev's authority is sufficiently firm to allow him to shrug off opposition to any settlement he may choose to sign. His commitment to finding a solution stems from a perception of the unresolved conflict as the greatest remaining obstacle to Azerbaijan's independence and prosperity, now that internal enemies have been overcome, the oil boom is gathering pace, and international configurations are more favourable than in the past. Nor should it be forgotten that Azerbaijan would reap substantial benefits from reopening the borders with Armenia in terms of communications and trade with Nakhichevan and Turkey. Any solution which formally preserved Azerbaijan's territorial integrity and allowed refugees to return to their homes would be unlikely to arouse too much popular or political resistance to the current well-entrenched regime.

In Armenia the commitment to an early settlement is less assured. Robert Kocharian has reiterated the Armenian government's commitment to peaceful negotiation, but there is a significant difference between his position and that of Ter-Petrosian. The latter saw a settlement in Karabagh as essential for Armenia's economic development and therefore as an urgent priority, while Kocharian argues that Armenia and Karabagh can develop economically even without a settlement (see Chapter 5). Most parties and public opinion seem to side with Kocharian's tougher stance and rhetoric, but it is interesting that Karabagh was scarcely an issue in the 1998 presidential election campaign, when social and economic problems topped the list of voters' concerns.

Ultimately, the Karabagh Armenians have the most to gain from a settlement. An internationally guaranteed peace that gives them self-government, unrestricted communications with Armenia and the advantages of a free trade zone would appear an attractive proposition, but it is in Stepanakert that opposition to the proposals for a settlement is strongest. The principal reason is a deep distrust of Baku and of the value of international undertakings. That distrust has been nurtured by Karabagh's exclusion from parts of the negotiation process and has only hardened as Yerevan and Stepanakert have become more isolated. Other factors also contribute to Karabagh intransigence. There is a perhaps exaggerated confidence in Karabagh's military capability to defend the status quo, and a belief that the longer the current stalemate continues the more firmly entrenched Karabagh's independence will become. Moreover, Karabagh's economic situation is not too dire, at least by comparison with Abkhazia's. Subventions from Armenia's budget, aid from the diaspora (notably for the construction of a new Stepanakert to Goris road through the Lachin corridor), and income from trade with Iran, Azerbaijan (largely contraband petroleum products) and Armenia (where the Karabagh mafia is playing a growing role), all help to keep the republic afloat. The leadership is a clear beneficiary of this highly controlled economy which owes little to the productive output of the territory or its people. Vested economic interests (in both Karabagh and Armenia) in maintaining the status quo cannot be ignored as an obstacle to a settlement.

In the long run the biggest obstacle lies in the isolation and suspicion of the Karabagh Armenians. This can only be gradually overcome by placing greater emphasis on Stepanakert in international initiatives, by making the benefits of peace apparent to the Karabagh leadership and people, and by seeking to build confidence between Karabagh Armenians and Azeris. In a state of blockade confidence-building faces special difficulties. One component, however, must be the opening of official contacts between Baku and Stepanakert. Azerbaijani objections to direct talks increasingly seem artificial and counterproductive. Baku will need to be on speaking terms with Stepanakert after any settlement, so it would surely be to the advantage of both parties to begin to develop a relationship sooner rather than later.

South Ossetia

Development of the conflict
The roots of the conflict in South Ossetia also reach deep into history, with Ossetes and Georgians advancing mutually exclusive historical claims to the disputed territory.[35] Like Karabagh, South Ossetia witnessed bloody conflict in the period between the Russian Revolution and the establishment of Soviet power, and also like Karabagh the present dispute owes much to the 1920s Soviet border delimitation which established South Ossetia as an autonomous region (*oblast*) within the Republic of Georgia. Georgians criticized the delimitation as an example of Moscow's strategy of divide and rule, while Ossetes were dissatisfied

with their subjection to Tbilisi and with the separation of the Ossetian people, of whom the larger part (some 350,000 in 1989) live in the North Ossetian Autonomous Republic of the Russian Federation.

In 1989–91 Georgian and Ossetian nationalists took advantage of the freedoms of glasnost to press their claims, Georgians asserting the primacy of Tbilisi's authority and Georgian language and culture throughout the republic, while Ossetes responded by emphasizing their autonomy and links with North Ossetia.

The dispute escalated on both constitutional and conflictual levels. The South Ossetian Soviet adopted a declaration of sovereignty in August 1990, and in September requested recognition from Moscow as an independent subject of the USSR. It organized elections in December of the same year and the new parliament subordinated itself directly to Moscow.[36] Tbilisi excluded regional parties (including Ossetian ones) from national elections and in December 1990 abolished South Ossetia as a distinct administrative entity. In a January 1992 referendum the South Ossetian leadership claimed a 99 per cent vote in favour of joining the Russian Federation and uniting with North Ossetia.

Serious fighting started at the end of 1990 and gradually intensified, with Ossetian militias fighting Georgian militias, interior ministry troops and the National Guard, and also drawing in Soviet interior ministry forces. Initial fighting was concentrated in the regional capital, Tskhinvali, from which the Ossetes expelled the Georgians, who then besieged and bombarded them from the surrounding hills. There was also fighting in villages around Tskhinvali and over road links, with Georgians trying to interdict the road to North Ossetia, while the Ossetes sought to cut communications between Georgian villages and the rest of Georgia. The fighting continued during the coup against Gamsakhurdia and for some months after Shevardnadze's return to Georgia in March 1992. The Ossetes eventually gained the upper hand, thanks at least in part to arms and direct support from the Russian military. The fighting was accompanied by serious human rights abuses against civilians.[37]

Most of the Georgian population of South Ossetia was displaced to Georgia, though some villages north of Tskhinvali remain Georgian-populated and outside Ossetian control. At least half of the roughly 100,000 Ossetes living in other parts of Georgia emigrated to South or North Ossetia, while a significant number emigrated from South to North Ossetia to escape the fighting and seek better economic conditions.[38]

In June 1992 a cease-fire was signed, to be supervised by a combined Russian, Georgian and Ossetian PKF under a Joint Control Commission

(JCC). The cease-fire was not negotiated under the auspices of any international organization, but was essentially an arrangement between Russia and the conflicting parties, though North Ossetia also is represented on the JCC. Russians have been the largest contingent of the PKF and have carried the brunt of the operations.

The OSCE has had a resident mission in Georgia since late 1992. Its original mandate was to promote negotiations between conflicting parties in Georgia, but in March 1994 the mandate was extended to include monitoring the peace-keeping operation in South Ossetia. In spite of a number of incidents and violations of the cease-fire, and failings on the part of the PKF, the force has generally fulfilled its function, with the result that by February 1997 hostility and tension had subsided to a level which allowed the JCC to agree a reduction in the PKF presence. The OSCE's mission has been low-profile but apparently effective, not only allaying Georgian suspicions of Russian peace-keeping, but also acting as a liaison point and source of information for NGOs working in the region. The cease-fire and the relative calm have allowed the reopening of communications and the movement of people and goods, as well as the initiation of a number of confidence-building measures by the OSCE and NGOs.[39]

Negotiations and prospects

As a result, negotiations between the parties, under Russian auspices but supported by the OSCE mission, have been conducted in a more positive atmosphere than in the case of the Abkhazian and Karabagh conflicts. In addition to official discussions, there has been a development of civil dialogue providing a background conducive to progress in negotiations. In May 1996 the parties signed a memorandum on refraining from the threat of force, solving the refugee problem, gradual demilitarization and continuing dialogue and negotiations. The parties subsequently empowered delegations to discuss a comprehensive settlement.

These positive developments notwithstanding, a comprehensive settlement has not yet been reached, with negotiations deadlocked over the issue of status and the division of powers and responsibilities between Tbilisi and Tskhinvali. In part this may reflect a reluctance on the part of the Ossete leadership to accept a settlement which might leave them with more limited rights than may be granted in subsequent settlements of other Caucasian conflicts, in Abkhazia, Karabagh or Chechenia. The Georgian constitution's reference to asymmetrical federalism reinforces this concern.

So far there has not been an extensive movement back to their homes of people displaced by the war. The issue of security for returning refugees and the mechanism for compensating those whose homes cannot be returned to them present serious difficulties, in spite of the fact that reciprocal arrangements could be made – Georgian refugees from South Ossetia are balanced by Ossete refugees from Georgia.

Six years after the cease-fire the situation remains fragile. The maintenance of stability in Georgia and the continuation of the current moderate leadership in South Ossetia are essential conditions for further progress. If these conditions continue, then the prospects for solution seem quite good, especially if confidence-building measures are sustained. Economic incentives are also being proffered, with the OSCE mission identifying reconstruction projects and the UNDP and European Union making funding commitments.

Abkhazia

Development of the conflict

Abkhazia is almost twice the size of Karabagh and more than twice the size of South Ossetia.[40] Its population before the current conflict was over half a million, more than three times that of Karabagh and five times that of South Ossetia. Moreover, Abkhazia is a far more strategic territory than the other two disputed regions, straddling Georgia's only rail and an important road link to Russia, as well as containing half of Georgia's coastline, including the best tourist resorts, rich agricultural and mineral resources and a major power station. The Abkhaz themselves, however, numbered only 93,000 in 1989, a mere 1.8 per cent of Georgia's population and 18 per cent of the population of Abkhazia. Some 45 per cent of the population was Georgian,[41] while Armenians and Russians between them accounted for nearly 30 per cent.

The origins of the conflict, once again, are rooted in history and in incompatible exclusive claims to the territory by the conflicting parties.[42] As with Karabagh and South Ossetia the 1920s–1930s Soviet border delimitation and administrative arrangements are a source of grievance for both sides. Abkhazia was created as a separate Soviet Socialist Republic in 1921, but was joined with Georgia in a confederative Union Treaty later the same year. The 1925 constitution of Abkhazia confirmed both the unification with Georgia and Abkhazia's sovereignty. Abkhazia's status was downgraded and it was formally incorporated into Georgia as an autonomous republic only in 1931.[43]

The Gorbachev period brought the fears and ambitions of both Georgians and Abkhaz into the open. The latter saw their survival threatened by Tbilisi's encouragement of Georgian immigration to Abkhazia and its assertion of the primacy of Georgian language and culture and of Tbilisi's authority. They countered with increasingly forceful articulation of their autonomy and by reinforcing their links with Russia and the north Caucasian peoples. Georgians for their part feared Abkhaz ambitions directed at the dismemberment of Georgia, saw Moscow's hand in their rejection of Tbilisi's authority and resented the preferential treatment Moscow accorded the Abkhaz – it allocated some two-thirds of party and government positions within the republic to them, though they accounted for only about one-sixth of its population. From the 1930s onwards there had been sporadic Abkhaz protests against their subjugation under Tbilisi's authority and against the policy of Georgianization. In the 1960s and 1970s there had been requests to Moscow for a return to the 1920s status quo.

From 1988 relations between Sukhumi and Tbilisi deteriorated steadily, as did Abkhaz–Georgian inter-ethnic relations. In August 1990 the Abkhazian Supreme Soviet declared Abkhazia's sovereignty, and in July 1992 voted to return to the 1925 constitution. In 1991 the Abkhazian authorities defied Tbilisi to hold a referendum on Gorbachev's proposed new union treaty. The result was a large majority in favour of joining the proposed reconstituted Soviet Union as an autonomous republic.[44]

The main fighting in the Abkhazian war took place in 1992–3. In August 1992 the Georgian State Council ordered the National Guard into Abkhazia, ostensibly in order to suppress looting and sabotage and rescue some kidnapped officials. Tengiz Kitovani, the National Guard commander, was later blamed for the decision to send troops into Sukhumi. This operation was accompanied by wanton violence and extensive and serious human rights abuses against Abkhaz and other non-Georgian civilians. Revenge atrocities were subsequently perpetrated by Abkhaz troops.[45] In response to the Georgian attack, the Abkhaz leader, Vladislav Ardzinba, mobilized support from the Confederation of Caucasian Peoples, with Chechen fighters playing a major role in subsequent operations. The Abkhaz also benefited from Russian military support channelled through the Russian bases in Abkhazia at Gudauta and Bombora, though the scale of that support and the level at which it was authorized remain disputed.[46] The reinforced Abkhaz forces now enjoyed a clear military advantage and in March 1993 they launched an offensive which, though punctuated by cease-fire agreements, culminated in September in a decisive Abkhaz victory with all Georgian troops and the entire Georgian population expelled from almost the whole of Abkhazia. This left the Abkhaz in control of Abkhazia (some 12.5 per cent of the territory of the Republic of Georgia). The war is estimated to have claimed 4,000–8,000 casualties and caused massive economic damage.

Negotiations

Talks between the Georgians and the Abkhaz under Russian and UN auspices (the UN had been active in Georgia since autumn 1992) resulted in December 1993 in the signing of a memorandum of understanding, and in May 1994 in a cease-fire agreement and agreement on the deployment of a CIS PKF to be monitored by a UN force (UNOMIG). These arrangements have been in place ever since, with some 1,500 (Russian) peace-keepers (the force was initially 2,500 strong) and nearly 150 UNOMIG observers patrolling a 24-km-wide security zone.

Negotiations with mediation by the UN (held in Geneva under the Friends of the Secretary General on Georgia Group, comprising the United States, Germany, France and the UK) and Russia have continued. Increasing pressure has been exerted on the Abkhaz leadership to make concessions. Russia closed its land border with Abkhazia in late 1994, and imposed a naval blockade in response to the imposition of sanctions by the CIS in 1996.[47]

The tense and frequently violated cease-fire has given urgency to efforts to negotiate a settlement. The major negotiating role has been played by Moscow. Its bouts of shuttle diplomacy have borne fruit in a series of high-level meetings between Georgian and Abkhaz officials, culminating in a significant step forward in August 1997 when Shevardnadze and Ardzinba met in Tbilisi and signed an agreement renouncing the use of force.

Georgians have accused the PKF of failing to fulfil its mandate, since the return of the approximately 200,000 Georgians displaced from Abkhazia has not been facilitated or secured. Tbilisi has several times threatened to refuse to extend the PKF mandate for this reason. Georgians are also unhappy with the Russian monopolization of the PKF. They see Russia, particularly the Russian military, as having actively supported the Abkhaz during hostilities (including those in 1998), and therefore as unfit to act as impartial peace-keepers. Finally, the Georgians complain that the current status quo entrenches Abkhaz territorial gains and ethnic cleansing, and that the PKF contributes to this process.

Well-equipped Georgian paramilitaries, the White Legion and the Forest Brothers, have been active in the Gali region in the south of

Abkhazia. They have targeted Russian peace-keepers as well as Abkhaz police in their mission to fight to defend returning Georgian refugees. More than sixty peace-keepers have been killed in ambushes or by mines. These guerrillas' financial and logistical backing remains obscure – Tbilisi denies that they are supported by the government, but they have links with the Abkhaz parliament in exile (comprising Georgian representatives from the old Abkhaz Soviet), whose leader is on Georgia's Security Council.[48] The guerrillas have become an important element in a tense and volatile situation in and around the security zone. Their attacks triggered extensive fighting in May 1998, which caused dozens, if not hundreds, of casualties, again including civilians, and forced some 40,000 Georgians who had returned to the Gali region (the pre-conflict population there had been some 85,000, over 90 per cent Georgian) to flee their homes for a second time.

The Abkhaz also have reason for discontent. They believe that the Georgian government provides backing to the White Legion. They feel threatened by the prospect of a large-scale return of refugees and resent the economic blockade to which they have been subjected and which, they argue, makes the return of refugees impossible. They accuse the international mediators, including the Russians, of bias in favour of the Georgians.[49]

Moscow for its part is increasingly dissatisfied with the current arrangement, which does not discernibly serve Russian interests, but damages Russia's standing with both parties to the conflict, exposes it to criticism in international forums (such as the CIS) for the failings of its peace-keeping operations, and is unpopular at home, where there is little appreciation of the need to lose Russian lives in this intractable conflict. Finally, resource constraints compel the Russian government to look closely at all military commitments. So far Moscow still considers the PKF worthwhile, or at least preferable to the alternatives of a UN, OSCE, NATO or Ukrainian PKF, but that view is not certain to be sustained, especially if the PKF suffers increasing casualties.

Prospects

In considering the prospects for a settlement, two issues stand out.

- The question of the future status of Abkhazia remains intractable. Tbilisi argues for some kind of federative arrangement, as allowed under the Georgian constitution. However little actual control Tbilisi may exercise over Sukhumi, it wants Abkhazia recognized as a subordinate part of a single Georgian state, as has been the situation since 1931. The Abkhaz argue for a confederation between two equal partners on the pattern of the 1921 and 1925 arrangements. There are differences within the Abkhaz leadership, but all insist on real self-government and internal sovereignty.[50]

- The other major obstacle to agreement is the return of Georgian refugees. To date the Abkhaz have kept the rate of return to a trickle by carefully vetting returnees. They did not, however, prevent the unofficial spontaneous return of some 40,000 Georgians to the Gali region (see above). Returnees have complained of abuse at the hands of Abkhaz police, prompting the intervention of the Georgian guerrillas to protect them. This in turn tends to escalate conflict and reinforce Abkhaz fears that the Georgian returnees will be a fifth column preparing the way for an eventual Georgian reconquest.

The great majority of Georgian refugees from Abkhazia live in poor conditions, many in central Tbilisi. They form an outspoken lobby, with their own parliament and government in exile. While the Georgian government makes use of the refugees to bolster its claims and gain international sympathy, the refugees are not a pliable force and have consistently pressured Shevardnadze through parliament and sympathetic media to adopt a tougher stance, if not launch a military reconquest.

Abkhaz reluctance to accommodate Georgian returnees is not only related to concern about Georgian militias and the possibility of renewed fighting. In the long run the greatest threat is that the Abkhaz could again become a small minority in their own land. Even if they are guaranteed special places in governments and legislatures in Tbilisi and Sukhumi, no post-Soviet constitution will allow them the same disproportionate representation that they enjoyed in the late Soviet period. This has led Abkhaz leaders to assert that they must never again allow themselves to become a minority – with a clear implication that the full return of refugees will not be permitted. One solution that has been proposed (the so-called Bosnian model) is to redraw Abkhazia's internal borders to create Abkhaz and Georgian enclaves, but this has been rejected by both Tbilisi and Sukhumi.

If the status and refugee issues present tough problems, there are also strong incentives for a resolution. For the Georgian government the current situation is politically difficult, exposing it to continuous domestic criticism for its alleged weakness and failure to secure the rights of Georgian refugees. It is economically damaging, cutting off the best transport routes to Russia, discouraging investment in the whole of Georgia and preventing the rebirth of the potentially lucrative tourist trade. Finally, it complicates relations with Russia and leaves Georgia exposed to manipulation by forces in Russia.

For the Abkhaz too there are strong incentives for settlement. The republic's economy is in ruins because of war damage, the emigration of most of the skilled labour force and the economic blockade. The population is reduced to less than half its pre-war level, with a disproportionate share of young and old and of women; many of those of working age have left to seek employment. Abkhazia's strategic location and rich mineral, agricultural and leisure resources offer good economic opportunities once peace is agreed.[51] A project to construct a pipeline across Abkhazia to link the two main Black Sea oil terminals (Novorossiisk in Russia and Supsa in Georgia) for the future export of Caspian oil has gained approval in Sukhumi.

The fact that both Georgian and Abkhaz leaderships have more than once pulled back from the brink of renewed hostilities and have allowed the PKF to continue to operate suggests that both parties recognize that they have more to gain from peace than from renewed fighting. The obstacles to a settlement remain very great, especially in the absence of confidence-building measures and regular human and economic interaction. The risk of a further major outbreak of fighting between the Abkhaz and the Georgian guerrillas, possibly escalating to more widespread resumption of hostilities, cannot be excluded.

Summing up

The three Caucasian states have all been confronted with exceptionally difficult security challenges. They have had to respond to secessionist conflicts both at home and across their borders. They have had to manoeuvre among shifting international interests and policies in the region, with those of Russia presenting particular problems for Azerbaijan and Georgia. And against this background of immediate threats and challenges, they have had to begin to develop long-term security policies and military capabilities.

In spite of hesitant beginnings and the adoption of unrealistic policies by Baku and Tbilisi, the achievements have been considerable: all three states have gone a long way towards establishing political control and unified command structures over their military and security forces. They have also begun to diversify security relations and have made some progress towards tackling potential internal 'hotspots' before they break out into open conflict. At the same time all three countries remain vulnerable to both traditional and non-traditional security threats.

The conflicts over Karabagh, South Ossetia and Abkhazia have been central to the security concerns of all three states and their stabilization has itself been an important achievement. The cease-fires have greatly enhanced the region's security, and for Azerbaijan and Georgia at least, economic development and growing contacts with the outside world are possible even if the current stalemate persists for some time. Having won the war, the secessionist republics and Armenia currently risk losing the peace, with their opportunities for trade, economic development, travel and international contacts constrained to varying degrees. If the 'frozen' state of the conflicts marks a great improvement on the period of open warfare, it falls far short of resolution and continues to threaten the security and stability of the entire region.

Only in South Ossetia is the situation reasonably calm, giving little reason to fear a renewed outbreak of fighting. In Karabagh and particularly in Abkhazia the cease-fire is fragile and subject to frequent, sometimes serious, violations. For the moment it appears that none of the parties sees an advantage in escalating the regular incidents into full-scale war, but it cannot be assumed that this situation will last, particularly as the military balance shifts, as current leaders are replaced by others who may be more hard-line, and as the dead-end situation of the secessionists becomes increasingly apparent.

While each of the conflicts presents a somewhat different configuration of broadly similar ideological, constitutional, security, humanitarian and economic issues, the greatest single obstacle to a peaceful resolution in every case seems to be the underlying problem of inter-ethnic mistrust and deep suspicion by the secessionists of the Azerbaijani and Georgian governments. Without a fundamental change in those attitudes, it is unlikely that the secessionists will be willing to sacrifice military strength for the uncertain benefits of accommodation with governments and peoples whose ultimate intentions they believe to be hostile, if not genocidal. To effect such a change requires inter-ethnic dialogue, and international encouragement and incentives.

These are under way in South Ossetia, where the prospects for an early settlement appear relatively good, in spite of a persistent stalemate on the constitutional issue. In Abkhazia there has been direct official dialogue and some confidence-building measures. Blockade, however, precludes the development of normal human and economic relations between the parties. It is likely that contacts will have to be developed over a considerable period before agreement can be reached, the great economic incentives for a resolution notwithstanding. In the case of Karabagh there is no official bilateral contact and there has been almost nothing in the way of dialogue or confidence-building between Azeris and Karabagh Armenians. A resolution will remain a remote possibility while Baku believes that it can negotiate a settlement with Yerevan alone, using economic instruments to pressure or entice Stepanakert and Yerevan into a compromise, and while Stepanakert (and perhaps Yerevan) deludes itself that its military superiority is assured and its economic development can be achieved in spite of blockade.

Chapter 4

International relations

Locating the Caucasus in the international system

The three small, weak and conflict-ridden Caucasian states (with a combined population of around 15 million) are located at the junction of three much larger and more powerful states: the Russian Federation (population approximately 150 million), Turkey (population approximately 63.5 million) and Iran (population approximately 60 million). Relations between these powerful states have included, and continue to include, strong elements of rivalry (in the past, territorial wars for possession of the Caucasus, for example) as well as of common interest (today, in varying degrees, economic relations, strategic interests and concern for regional stability serve to bring them together). Shifts in the policies of and relations between these three have a powerful and uncontrollable impact on the Caucasian states. The collapse of the Soviet Union and the opening of the Caucasian republics' southern and western borders brought to an end a long period of relative stability and low intensity in international relations. The current situation is one of flux, with Caucasian state and sub-state actors, Russia, Turkey and Iran, as well as several more remote actors (notably the United States and Europe), involved in developing a new pattern of international relations. After nearly a decade, this process is still confused, with uncertainty reigning over a number of crucial questions:

- How far and for how long will Russian power in the Caucasus decline?
- Will the Caucasian states take advantage of Russian weakness to realign themselves within the Western hegemonic system?

- Will the Caucasian states be able to identify common interests and develop regional cooperation to bolster their sovereignty and security?
- How far will Turkey and Iran be able to seize the opportunity to extend their influence in the region?
- Will other external actors, such as the United States, Europe, international organizations and multinational corporations, develop a strong interest and presence in the region and come to play an important role in shaping its future?
- Will the new pattern of Caucasian international relations develop towards the domination of a single power (as has been the case during the last two centuries of Russian rule), towards an equilibrium in which all or most actors consider their key interests satisfied in a positive-sum outcome, or towards a more confrontational pattern, in which states, or blocs of states, engage in zero-sum competition with eventual winners and losers?

This chapter addresses these questions first by considering the principal factors that bear on the interests and perceptions of the sets of actors involved in the developing international relations of the Caucasian states, and second by examining in turn the specific interests and policies of those actors.

Factors

Strategic geographical location

In addition to being the point where the borders of Russia, Turkey and Iran meet, the Caucasus is a meeting point or bridge or borderland in several other ways. This central characteristic of the region serves both to underpin and to complicate the Caucasian states' international relations.

In terms of culture, language and religion the Caucasus is exceptionally diverse and thoroughly meshed with the surrounding countries and peoples. Its ethnic and linguistic composition is complex and fragmented (these characteristics were even more marked before the Soviet period), with peoples belonging to the Caucasian (both northern and southern branches), the Indo-European (both Armenian and Iranian branches) and Turkic language families, as well as significant communities of Jews, Greeks, Russians and others distributed across the region, with little regard for national and administrative boundaries. With the exception of the Georgians, each of these ethnic groups maintains links with linguistically and ethnically close relatives abroad. Some examples of how this has affected the processes of nation- and state-building, and the course of the conflicts, have already been mentioned in Chapters 2 and 3, but those examples form part of a wider pattern, in which Armenians maintain close links with and rely on the support of the worldwide Armenian diaspora, in which the Azeri Turks seek to develop their social and cultural links with the Azeris of Iran, while also looking to Turkey as a natural ally, in which Russians expect protection from the Russian state, and in which the several peoples separated by the Caucasus range and the border of the Russian Federation try to maintain links with and offer support to ethnic kin (e.g. the Abkhaz with the Adyghe and other north Caucasians, the North Ossetes with the South Ossetes, the Lezgins across the Azerbaijani–Russian border, the North Caucasian peoples with their diaspora kin in Turkey).

For external states, these cultural, linguistic and ethnic links can serve to create a consciousness of obligation or responsibility to become involved in the affairs of the region – a consciousness which is often reinforced by public opinion and lobbying by diaspora communities. They may also provide pretexts for interference and justification for policies which would be hard to argue on the basis of legitimate national interest.

The religious profile of the Caucasus also is heterogeneous. While it can broadly be seen as a borderland between the Christian and Muslim worlds, other religions too are represented (by Yazidi Kurds, Europe's only indigenous Buddhists, and Jews, for example). Both Christianity and Islam are present in a variety of sects and subdivisions. The Russian and Georgian Orthodox and the Armenian Apostolic churches, as well as Russian Old Believers, Roman Catholics and more recently arrived Protestant churches are all to be found, while both the main sects of Islam, Sunni and Shi'i, and other religious currents – such as *wahhabi* fundamentalism, Sufi mysticism – have their adherents among the Muslims of the Caucasus.

Like the region's ethnic and linguistic diversity, its religious character also plays some role in suggesting and consolidating international relations. In the past religion was an important factor in the Caucasian peoples' international orientation, with the Christian Armenians and Georgians appealing to Russia for protection, while the Muslim peoples looked for support to Sunni Turkey or Shi'i Iran. In the sixteenth and seventeenth centuries the sectarian frontier between Sunni and Shi'i Islam lay across the Caucasus, and the wars between the Ottoman (Turkish) and Safavi (Iranian) empires were waged in the name of religion. One consequence of those wars was that the majority of Azeris became at least nominal adherents of the same Shi'i sect as the Iranians. In the contemporary period, neither ruling elites nor public debate have, for the most part, laid heavy emphasis on religion in either politics or international relations. However, as suggested in Chapters 2 and 3, religion has its place in the nation-building projects of both Armenia and Georgia (particularly in the late Soviet and Gamsakhurdia periods), while even in Azerbaijan the president's inauguration includes a blessing from the most senior Muslim cleric. Several of the Caucasian conflicts have a sectarian dimension. Russian and Western sympathies for the Armenian cause in the early days of the Karabagh conflict following the Sumgait pogrom were at least partly conditioned by the perception of Armenians as Christian victims of Muslim fanatics. Azerbaijan's use of Afghan *mojaheddin* mercenaries in the fighting and its mobilization of support through the Organization of Islamic Conference (OIC) had a similar sectarian dimension.

For states with a strong religious ideology, such as Iran and Saudi Arabia, and for non-state actors (churches, foundations, NGOs and charities) and international organizations of a religious character, religious links with the region have helped to identify interests and decide affiliations.

The Caucasus has also been seen as a meeting place of Europe to the west and Asia to the east, of the Middle East to the south and Russia and the Eurasian steppe to the north. While these entities may appear vaguely symbolic rather than susceptible to precise definition, they are of considerable significance in informing the identities and international orientation of the Caucasian states and peoples, as well as in shaping the way the Caucasus is perceived by outsiders. Debate over where the Caucasus region 'belongs' in the broadest sense has been and will continue to be an important factor in the region's international relations. This debate is going on among the Caucasian peoples (as well as among neighbouring peoples), as they seek to define where their cultural affinities and national interests lie, and how these should affect their international orientation. It will also influence decisions about the limits of the possible extension to the Caucasus of European organizations and institutions, about the acceptability or otherwise of the Caucasus falling into any state's sphere of influence, about Caucasian states' participation and role in regional international organizations, such as the CIS, the Economic Cooperation Organization (ECO) and the Black Sea Economic Cooperation (BSEC). In the Cold War period the Caucasus also marked the southern frontier between NATO and the Warsaw Pact, a factor which will be discussed in the next section on security.

The Caucasus is also a physical meeting point for several economic regions, and historically has had an important role as a land bridge traversed by many important east–west and north–south trade routes. This will be discussed below, in the section on economic factors.

Finally, the Caucasus is not only a meeting point, but also a melting-pot, and the prospects for it to develop a sense of regional identity and to begin to function as a region in its relations with the rest of the world will depend in part on the extent to which Caucasians become conscious of what they have in common, and what distinguishes them from their linguistic or ethnic or religious fellows in Russia, Turkey, Iran or further afield.[1] 'Caucasianness' remains an elusive quality that has scarcely appeared on the agenda of the last two centuries, when political and cultural aspirations have been directed towards ethnic particularism, the development of distinct national cultures and exclusive claims for national territories. Yet at a popular and informal level there is a wide recognition among Armenians, Azeris and Georgians and the region's other peoples that Caucasians, in spite of their divisions and animosities, have a great deal in common, in terms of temperament and social and material culture. Cultural history offers support to this consciousness, although there have been very few members of the modern cultural elite who have recognized this fact (the most striking exception being the artist and film director Sergei Paradjanov). Soviet popular culture certainly recognized Caucasians as a generic group, although one which was identified with negative characteristics in the eyes of most Slavs.

Sovereignty, security and stability

Chapter 3 discussed security issues and conflicts in the context of the states and peoples of Armenia, Azerbaijan and Georgia, but this issue has also been one of the principal factors shaping the international relations of the region. In fact, insofar as the Caucasus has impinged on international interest in the last decade, it has been primarily through conflict and violence and the weakness of the new state system in the region. The Caucasus has acquired a reputation second only to the Balkans as a crucible for intractable ancient hatreds and regional and international rivalries.

For the Caucasian states and peoples – both the majority nationalities and the secessionist minorities – the most important international dimension to the conflicts has been the balance of external support and sympathy for the parties to each conflict and for competing proposals for their resolution. For all, an important aspect of this has been the quest for international recognition and support for their independence. All have attempted to maximize external support through bilateral state-to-state relations and international forums, and by cultivating links with a variety of sub-state institutions and lobbies. For external actors this has posed the question of how to respond to such appeals, and whether offering recognition or support to one or other of the parties to a conflict can help to further national interests. For neighbouring powers, it has been open to question whether the establishment of three viable sovereign states in the Caucasus is a more favourable outcome than the maintenance of the status quo of fragmented and dependent state and sub-state entities. More remote actors have not doubted the desirability of real independence for Armenia, Azerbaijan and Georgia, but questions remain over what are desirable models for state development in the region and how to support them.

More broadly, however, the Caucasian conflicts and the general volatility and instability of the region have posed a number of threats to international security in general and to the security of neighbouring states in particular. The danger of a spill-over of fighting has affected the Russian Federation, Iran and Turkey (the last more indirectly, through its treaty obligations as a guarantor of Nakhichevan's status). Refugees have been another source of concern, with Russia absorbing a large number of fugitives from Caucasian conflicts, and Iran in 1993–4 facing the possibility of a major influx of Azeri refugees.

Another threat affecting all the countries of the region has been the possibility of direct impact or indirect knock-on effect between the conflicts and nationality issues in the Caucasus and in neighbouring states. The most acute example is the linkage of Georgia's wars with inter-ethnic conflicts and tensions in the North Caucasus; but the Lezgin issue, the possibility of support reaching the Chechen secessionists via Azerbaijan, the risk that nationalist appeals from Azerbaijan might stir dissatisfaction among Iran's Azeri population, and even the possibility of Turkey's Kurdish separatists gaining support or finding refuge in Armenia have all caused anxiety at one time or another. Public opinion in Russia, Turkey and Iran is interested in the Caucasian conflicts and has periodically exerted an influence on or constrained the options of governments and policy-makers.

In responding to these threats, neighbouring states have been obliged to take an interest and engage in the Caucasus region, whether by asserting their security interests and taking steps to protect them, or by overt or covert intervention in Caucasian politics or conflicts in order to try to achieve favourable outcomes, or by acting as mediators or peacemakers. This engagement by interested neighbouring states has become an important aspect of the conflicts and one which the parties to them have themselves sought to exploit to their advantage, by encouraging the intervention of friendly powers or expressing preference for sympathetic mediators.

On a wider level, the persistent Caucasian conflicts have demanded a response from the international community. They have tested the potential and capabilities for mediation and peace-keeping in the Caucasus of several international organizations, chief among them the United Nations, the OSCE and the CIS. Insofar as the CIS in general and the Caucasus in particular are viewed as part of Europe, they have challenged states and organizations concerned with European security in particular to engage and seek solutions.

In addition, the region's conflicts and instability have facilitated the development of the Caucasus as a base and corridor for various illicit trades, among them narcotics and arms (including at least the potential for the export of nuclear technology and material of ex-Soviet stock), and for international organized crime more generally. These have an impact first on the peoples of the region, though hitherto they have not figured high among the security concerns of the Caucasian states and secessionist republics (indeed there are persistent allegations that state or quasi-state actors are themselves directly engaged in or benefiting from these criminal activities). Such issues are, however, becoming increasingly important security priorities for the international community and the West, and provide another motivation for their engagement in the region.

The threat to regional and international stability posed by the Karabagh, Abkhazian and Ossetian conflicts is not, however, the only international security challenge posed by the Caucasus region. Irrespective of the level of internal stability of the region, it would have figured on the agenda of security issues of the post-Cold War world. As noted above, Turkey's border with Georgia and Armenia marked the southern border between NATO and the Warsaw Pact. The Caucasus figured in NATO–Warsaw Pact negotiations and treaties, notably in the CFF Treaty (see Chapter 3). The end of the Cold War and the break-up of the Warsaw Pact have, therefore, left the Caucasus in a strategic limbo.

If the Caucasus has not yet emerged as a principal subject of global military-strategic interest – debate over NATO enlargement in central Europe has kept attention focused in that direction – it retains its strategic importance. Whether the Caucasian countries remain within a Russian or CIS security system and military alliance, or break away from it individually or as a smaller regional security grouping, or attempt to attach themselves to a Western or European security system or military alliance are important questions for the Caucasian countries themselves, for Russia, for Iran and for the Western military-security establishment, not least for Turkey, whose own strategic significance for NATO is far from clear now that the Soviet threat has disappeared. Moreover, the three Caucasian countries and the major external players have deeply divergent views as to what would be the most desirable resolution of the current uncertainty. Strategic interests and even hints of old Cold War attitudes inform or at least colour the priorities and policies of the major powers. There is a possibility that their current quiet and undeclared competitive engagement in the region could be transformed into a more intense and undisguised strategic rivalry, in which the Caucasian states would figure rather as passive objects than active players. Alternatively, a new strategic balance could be reached, in which the fundamental interests of the regional and external powers would be respected while a situation is created in which multi-polar constructive engagement in the region is facilitated and the Caucasian countries' opportunities to develop diverse international links are maximized.

Economic factors

The Caucasian economies form the subject of Chapter 5, and the impact on the economies of Armenia, Azerbaijan and Georgia of foreign trade, investment, aid and loans will be discussed there. Here we are concerned only with those economic factors which feature prominently in the region's international relations, as major interests of the Caucasian states and external powers, and as objectives or levers in their foreign policies. Only two economic factors are of real significance in this regard: oil and transport. The two are closely connected, moreover, since the transport issue of the greatest international concern is the routing of pipelines to carry the oil and gas of the Caspian basin to global markets. Moreover both are closely related to the strategic factor discussed above, since in the modern global economy oil is a strategic economic resource, and control over or at least guaranteed access to oil supplies is a crucial state security concern. In the last couple of years the oil and pipelines factor has even overtaken conflict as the prime focus of international interest in the Caucasus, at least as expressed in the media.[2]

In terms of international relations the key characteristics of the oil factor in the Caucasus are that the only major potential reserves are located in fields in the Caspian Sea offshore from Azerbaijan. While Georgia has a small-scale petroleum industry and Armenia may have some gas resources, these are not of international significance. The

91

interest of the oil industry and the oil-importing countries in access to and development of petroleum resources of the Caucasian countries is, therefore, focused on Azerbaijan, the only state with the potential to use oil as a lever or lure in its foreign policy. It is also important to note that the Azerbaijani oil-fields are offshore, and that their ownership is disputed and will remain so until the five Caspian littoral states (among them Azerbaijan's two powerful neighbours, Russia and Iran) agree on a new legal regime for the sea and for sub-sea resources. International interest in oil, and the wealth generated by Azerbaijan's oil industry, have the potential over time to alter significantly the balance of power among the Caucasian states and among the external powers engaged in the region.

Transport and communications, like oil, are increasingly seen as strategic resources. During the Soviet period the Caucasus lost its historical role as a bridge for regional and intercontinental trade routes and became an isolated outpost of the Soviet Union, its economic links predominantly geared towards Russia and the other Soviet republics. The Caucasian economies and their neighbours, and the international economic system, have significant interests in the restoration of the role of the Caucasus as trade bridge, though both Caucasian and external players wish to maximize their own benefit from the development of the region's transport infrastructure. The routing of oil and gas pipelines is of particular importance. For both oil-importing and oil-exporting countries the security of pipelines from sabotage or political interference is a central concern, as also is the cost of transport. Routes that traverse stable and friendly states are, therefore, preferable. For potential transit countries, the attraction of securing the route for export pipelines lies in the transit dues, in the economic stimulus that will be provided by the construction, and in the future political leverage that the pipelines will provide. For commercial interests, ultimately only cost and security matter, though oil companies have to take account of the policies of their home governments. For Azerbaijan's oil there are three possible export directions, to the north via Russia to the Black Sea, to the west via Georgia to the Black Sea, or via Georgia (or Armenia or Iran) and Turkey to the Mediterranean, or via Iran to the Persian Gulf. The choice between these routes is a matter of great economic and strategic concern to Azerbaijan, to the oil-importing countries of the West, and to the potential transit countries. The fact that the first major international consortium developing offshore Caspian oil-fields is based in Azerbaijan (the Azerbaijan International Operating Company, AIOC), and the fact that it is already exporting oil and needs soon to secure additional pipeline capacity, have helped to bring the geo-economic and strategic aspects of the pipeline question to a head in the Caucasus. Several commentators have noted that oil and its transportation have the potential either to fuel regional economic development and positive-sum economic engagement of multiple international players (there have even been proposals for the deliberate routing of 'peace pipelines' through conflict zones to spread ethnic harmony and general prosperity), or to fan the flames of regional conflicts and zero-sum great-power rivalry.

What is true for pipelines is true also for road, rail, shipping and communications routes, though the choices present themselves less starkly than for pipelines as there is a more diverse provision. Nevertheless separate projects for developing the Caucasus region's transport infrastructure along either an east–west axis, as a transport corridor linking Europe and the Black Sea with the Caspian, Central Asia and East Asia, or north–south, linking Russia and the Black Sea with Iran, the Middle East and the Persian Gulf, have similar potential either to develop into complementary or even integrated schemes, or to vie for investment and traffic in a zero-sum competition.

Already the region's transport infrastructure (including pipelines) has become heavily politicized around the conflicts, with many of its existing internal and external links closed by continuing blockades imposed to put pressure on one or other party to the various conflicts. This fact suggests that developing infrastructure will not in itself promote a consciousness of common interests and shared benefits (the potential for these already exists in the current infrastructure, but lies unexploited in the closed roads, railways and pipelines). The historical record also is discouraging: in the past local conflict and great-power rivalry repeatedly frustrated plans to develop regional infrastructure, including pipelines for the export of Caspian oil.

Actors

This section will consider the international relations of the Caucasus region through the interests and policies of three concentric circles of actors, comprising an inner group of Caucasian state and sub-state actors, a second circle of regional powers bordering on the Caucasus and a third and outer circle of extra-regional countries and organizations.

Caucasian states: Armenia, Azerbaijan and Georgia
The foreign policies of all three Caucasian states have been dominated by relatively few central concerns: securing international recognition and support for their independence; cultivating friends and allies to meet their security needs, of which the most pressing have related to the Karabagh, Ossetian and Abkhazian conflicts (see Chapter 3); acquiring aid and economic assistance to meet immediate humanitarian and budget crises; and promoting long-term development of economic and infrastructure resources. Priorities and choices of strategies and tactics have been shaped by the specific configuration of internal, regional and international opportunities and constraints.

Following the break-up of the Soviet Union, the first priority of all three states was to gain international recognition and to take their place in the international community. In addition, all faced the urgent need to establish diplomatic and foreign policy institutions, which had not existed in the Soviet period. All quickly gained recognition from the major regional and global powers (though international recognition of Georgia's independence was delayed until Shevardnadze's return in March 1992), established diplomatic relations with a number of foreign states and became members of numerous international organizations, among them the United Nations, the Conference on Security and Cooperation in Europe, the International Monetary Fund, the World Bank, and the European Bank for Reconstruction and Development. All three are interested in deeper integration into the international, particularly European, political and economic system and are seeking membership of additional organizations, including the World Trade Organization and the Council of Europe (where they have observer status).

The declared principles underlying the foreign policies of all three states also have much in common. They emphasize the establishment of friendly, mutually beneficial and equal relations with foreign countries, particularly neighbouring states, the promotion of regional and international cooperation, particularly in the Caucasus and between the Caucasus and Europe. But the translation of these principles into policies, and the implementation of policies to gain tangible results have, in the differing national and international complexes of the three states, led to marked differences in the evolution of foreign policy.

In terms of foreign policy development Armenia appears as the odd one out among the three Caucasian states.[3] There are two main and inter-related reasons for this, one being that Yerevan has supported the claims of the Karabagh Armenian secessionists and has, therefore, found itself championing the cause of self-determination in an international system prejudiced towards upholding territorial integrity, and in marked contrast to Azerbaijan's and Georgia's insistence on territorial integrity; the other being Armenia's relatively benign view of Russia and its regional role, and its consequent prioritization of relations with Moscow and acquiescence in Russian proposals for the development of bilateral and multilateral relations (primarily in the CIS framework). Currently Armenia's pro-Russian foreign policy alignment seems well established, but the assumption that it has remained constant or is inevitable is mistaken.

During the year before independence, relations between Moscow and the ANM government in Yerevan had been severely strained and the Soviet government had backed Azerbaijan over the Karabagh conflict. In the period immediately after independence, Moscow for a time seemed inclined to relinquish its interests and positions in the Caucasus, obliging the Armenian government to imagine a future in which Russia could not be relied on for economic or security support. At this time Armenia was already blockaded by Azerbaijan and faced severe shortages of energy and food, so the most pressing priority was to secure supplies and ensure survival. International sympathy and aid were available, primarily from the United States and Europe, but delivering them to Armenia presented major difficulties. Landlocked Armenia's isolation was acute: routes through Georgia were subject to frequent interruption because of that country's internal strife, while the possibility of supplies through Iran was constrained by the fact that the West (the main source of aid and credit) was reluctant to use Iranian channels, and in any case there was no direct linkage of Armenian and Iranian road, rail, oil, gas or electricity infrastructure.

Turkey appeared the only channel for the acutely needed supplies, so Armenia's foreign policy in 1991–2 emphasized the establishment of normal relations with Ankara. Economic necessity and re-establishing old east–west trade links outweighed nationalist priorities. This was controversial in Armenia, and especially with many Armenians in the diaspora, whose perception of Turkey as the historical enemy was un-affected by the current exigencies of life in Armenia. President Levon Ter-Petrosian's refusal to make a diplomatic issue of the Genocide led to the resignation in 1992 of his diaspora-born foreign minister, Raffi Hovannisian, and to criticism from the nationalist opposition at home. Initially, however, the policy bore fruit and Armenia received vital food deliveries from Turkey and signed an agreement for the supply of electricity. Progress towards normalization faltered and supplies through Turkey dried up, however, as a result of Ankara's response to Armenian victories in the Karabagh war and Azerbaijan's appeals to it not to undermine the blockade of Armenia. Faced with a choice between support for the Karabagh Armenians and developing relations with Turkey, Yerevan gave priority to ethnic solidarity. In 1998 Robert Kocharian and his diaspora-born foreign minister, Vartan Oskanian, reaffirmed that choice, maintaining Ter-Petrosian's policy of seeking to normalize relations with Turkey, but not at the expense of the Karabagh Armenians. Moreover, there has been a further shift towards ethnic or nationalist priorities (this time of the diaspora rather than Karabagh), in that Yerevan now insists that the Genocide should be a subject for discussion in future dialogue with Turkey.

Ter-Petrosian continued to emphasize the importance of relations with Turkey and the correctness of his policy until his 1998 resignation, but the failure to achieve a breakthrough in relations obliged Yerevan to shift its focus in other directions. Relations with Iran, particularly trade relations and infrastructural developments such as the linking of road systems via a bridge across the River Aras and plans for gas and electricity lines, acquired greater significance. While unwelcome to Washington, they were uncontroversial at home and unopposed in Moscow. In the mid-1990s relations with Tbilisi received higher priority as Georgia's internal situation settled and the flow of goods and energy via Georgia became more reliable. Georgia's strategic and economic importance for Armenia as a transit route to the Black Sea and Russia (and around the Azerbaijani–Turkish blockade) has far outweighed any nationalist interest in supporting potential secessionism among Georgia's Armenian population (see Chapter 3). In all these areas sustaining the basic economic needs of the state and promoting trade links and regional cooperation have been the main priorities.

The most important shift, however, was a realignment towards Russia. This was partly a response to anxieties about the military threat posed by Turkey and Azerbaijan, but owed more to the realization that Russia had remained a far more important power in the region than had initially appeared to be the case. Although this prominent regional presence was not fully reflected in Moscow's foreign policy until the second half of 1993 (see below), the continued importance of Russian interests in the Caucasus was obvious much earlier and began to emerge in the context of the 1991–3 CIS negotiations over security. The strained relations between Russia and Azerbaijan at the time of Elchibey's APF government (1992–3) also presented Yerevan with an opportunity to be exploited. In 1992–3 the pattern of close Armenian–Russian relations was established, with the consolidation of links with Russian military staff and defence ministry personnel both locally and in Moscow, as well as between Ter-Petrosian and Yeltsin. Credit from Russia's Central Bank was vital to support Armenia's budget in this period. Armenian–Russian bilateral relations have been consolidated in a series of wide-ranging treaties and agreements, and Armenia has derived significant benefits from close relations with Moscow through support for its military development, government loans and energy supplies, and indirectly through the salaries remitted from Russia by the large number of Armenian economic migrants there. The emphasis on relations with Moscow has continued, regardless of Russia's declining power and prestige, following defeat in the Chechen war and the political and economic crises of 1998. Nevertheless, there are limits to the enthusiasm for deepening relations with Russia, and Yerevan has consistently rejected integrationist proposals that it considered likely to jeopardize its sovereignty, such as the CIS Customs Union or the Russia–Belarus Union. It has been keen to try to maintain balance in its foreign relations and sees such proposals as tying Armenia too closely into Russia's orbit, damaging its prospects for integration into European structures and the global economy, which are important long-term objectives.

The Karabagh conflict has exerted a powerful influence on Armenia's foreign policy. It contributed to the country's isolation, undermined the initiative to normalize relations with Turkey, and provided much of the rationale for the close relations with Russia, particularly in the military-security field. Inevitably it has frustrated the development of relations with Azerbaijan (though Ter-Petrosian insisted that Armenia did not consider Azerbaijan 'an enemy') and has complicated Armenia's partici-pation in projects for integration in the Caucasus region, including the possibility of benefiting as a transit country from the predicted Caspian oil boom. Conversely, statehood and international obligations have constrained Yerevan's position on the Karabagh issue. The government has significantly retracted from the 1988–90 calls for the unification of Armenia and Karabagh, and has refused to recognize Karabagh's independence – in spite of strong domestic pressure to do so. Neverthe-less Armenia still finds itself isolated at international forums, most notably at the 1996 Lisbon summit of the OSCE, and is unable to sustain policies on the basis of other interests if these are perceived to run counter to the Karabagh cause.

The Armenian diaspora has been a significant factor in Armenia's international relations. The link of ethnic solidarity has proved strong, and Yerevan has looked to diaspora communities for aid and economic support, and for influence on the public opinion and foreign policies of their countries. Diaspora Armenians have identified with the independence struggle of the Armenian homeland and have provided important support for Armenia in both regards, though it has not always been directed precisely towards Yerevan's priorities – diaspora initiatives have often focused on Karabagh. In spite of the ties of ethnic kinship and patriotism, for most of the period of Ter-Petrosian's presidency the relationship between the Armenian government and diaspora communities was troubled. Apart from differing priorities between homeland and diaspora Armenians (over relations with Turkey, for example), the fact that the ARF – one of the major political parties in the diaspora – was banned in Armenia from 1994 to 1998, and the ANM government's resistance to facilitating Armenian citizenship for diaspora Armenians, placed strains on relations and exacerbated long-standing divisions within the diaspora. Kocharian's government has given the Armenian diaspora and its concerns a higher priority.[5]

The development of Azerbaijan's[6] and Georgia's[7] international relations has been dominated by the priorities of establishing sovereignty and achieving satisfactory resolutions to internal conflicts. Government and popular opinion in both countries have seen Russia as representing a threat rather than a source of support in each of these two areas. The nationalist governments of Gamsakhurdia (1990–91) and Elchibey (1992–3) attempted a radical reorientation away from the Russian sphere of influence towards the West. Gamsakhurdia refused to make Georgia a member of the CIS, while Elchibey effectively withdrew Azerbaijan from the organization. In the case of Azerbaijan the rejection of Russia was combined with a strong emphasis on relations with Turkey, based on the pragmatic premise that Turkey provided the best means of access and introduction to Western political institutions and models and Western investors, as well as on the basis of ethnic and cultural kinship. The latter factor prompted Elchibey's expressions of support for the rights of the Azeri population of Iran, which alienated Tehran. In Georgia, in 1990–91 Gamsakhurdia appealed to the West for recognition and support, but this was not forthcoming prior to the collapse of the USSR, by which time the coup against him was already under way. He also sought to establish links with the Chechens and other north Caucasians interested in challenging Russian dominance.

The policies of both Baku and Tbilisi in the early 1990s failed. They succeeded in alienating Moscow and stimulating Russian backing for secessionists and other internal opponents, which contributed to the overthrow of both governments. But whereas Gamsakhurdia failed both to extricate Georgia from the means of Russian control, and to engage Western interest in Georgian independence, the Elchibey government in Azerbaijan did provide certain assets and set precedents for the foreign policy of Heydar Aliyev. The negotiated withdrawal of all Russian troops and border guards from Azerbaijan's territory helped Aliyev to develop independent foreign policy priorities, and at times to clash openly with Moscow (as over the Caspian Sea legal issue). Moreover, the APF government's initiation of 'oil diplomacy' – the exploitation of contracts for the development of the country's petroleum resources to create international economic interest in Azerbaijan's independence and stability and to win support for its position on the Karabagh dispute – has been adopted and continued under Aliyev.

In contrast to their nationalist predecessors, Aliyev and Shevardnadze have stressed their recognition of the continuing importance of Russia in the region and of the need for good relations with Moscow. They have mended relations with Moscow and in 1993 brought their countries into the CIS. Aliyev has welcomed Russian commercial participation in Azerbaijani oil contracts and the restoration of economic links. Shevardnadze's concessions have been more far-reaching: he accepted the presence of Russian military bases and border guards in Georgia and a leading role for Russia in peace-keeping operations in Abkhazia and South Ossetia. Both Baku and Tbilisi became more circumspect in their relations with the north Caucasian republics, avoiding any engagement that might provoke Russian concern. These concessions have led to a thaw with Moscow and what both Baku and Tbilisi view as a more balanced Russian position on their internal conflicts. Relations with Russia, however, have remained deeply ambivalent. The Georgian parliament and public opinion and the Azerbaijani opposition remain highly critical of Russia's role in the region and celebrate every hint of Russian weakness or withdrawal. Even senior government figures in both countries accuse forces in Moscow of supporting secessionists and plotters, and point to the presence in Moscow of several important opponents of their governments in exile (notwithstanding the fact that some, including Suret Huseinov, have been extradited). The Georgian parliament has delayed ratification of the military agreement with Russia until it is satisfied with the role of the Russian peace-keeping force in Abkhazia, while in 1998 Tbilisi succeeded in negotiating the withdrawal of Russian border guards. Azerbaijan protested vigorously about the

1997 revelation of Russia's massive arms supplies to Armenia.

Both Azerbaijan and Georgia have proved less than enthusiastic members of the CIS, rejecting integrationist initiatives that might compromise their sovereignty and repeatedly criticizing the organization as a vehicle for Russian ambitions and its failure to offer them effective support over Karabagh and Abkhazia. Increasingly Shevardnadze and Aliyev have used the CIS as a vehicle to criticize Russia's role in the post-Soviet space and to coordinate positions with other like-minded CIS governments. On various issues, Moldova, Ukraine, Uzbekistan and Kazakhstan have made common cause with Georgia and/or Azerbaijan. In the course of 1996 and 1997 a new alignment emerged involving initially Georgia, Ukraine and Azerbaijan, and subsequently also Moldova: this resulted in GUAM, an informal grouping committed to deepening cooperation in the political and economic fields and to the formation of a joint peace-keeping battalion.[8] While it has been stressed that GUAM is not directed against any state, there is no hiding the fact that it is an expression of its members' consciousness of shared strategic interests differing from those of Russia.

Outside the CIS also Tbilisi and Baku have attempted to diversify international links, consolidating cooperation with Turkey in the political, military-security and economic fields, and improving relations with Iran (although serious frictions remain in Azerbaijani–Iranian relations) and other foreign states in order to achieve wider international support for their statehood and territorial integrity. Another important priority for both has been the promotion of their role in a developing east–west transport and communications corridor, expressed in the European Union-sponsored TRACECA project, and in the projects for pipelines from Baku through Georgia to the Black Sea and Turkey.

The principal diplomatic efforts of both, however, have been directed towards the West. Baku has used participation in oil contracts to create economic interests in Azerbaijan for a range of Western countries (as well as Russia, Turkey and Japan), and has attempted to use oil interests to counter the influence of the Armenian lobby in the United States and France. Western oil companies and governments, while recognizing the issue as a matter for decision by the littoral states, have supported Azerbaijan's position on the legal status of the Caspian Sea. Georgia, without comparable economic attractions, has relied on the personal standing of Shevardnadze to cultivate Western sympathies, including through the Friends of the UN Secretary General on Georgia group of countries, and has also been an enthusiastic participant in NATO's PfP programme. Both Georgia and Azerbaijan have affirmed their conviction that they are part of Europe and have tried to accelerate their membership of European and Euro-Atlantic organizations.

In view of the parallels between their situations – unresolved internal conflicts with secessionists, perceptions of a Russian threat to their sovereignty, and a desire to develop political, economic and security ties with the West – the emergence of close bilateral relations between Azerbaijan and Georgia has been a natural development. These have been consolidated in a number of political and economic agreements, principally concerned with combating ethnic separatism and with developing mutually beneficial cooperation in the export to the West of Azerbaijan's oil.

As noted above, Georgia's bilateral relations with Armenia have also developed, with both sides interested in developing transport links across their territory from the Black Sea to Iran and the Persian Gulf. They have not, however, reached the same intensity as Azerbaijani–Georgian relations.

There have been a number of proposals and initiatives for multilateral Caucasian cooperation among the three states of the South Caucasus or between them and the north Caucasian republics of the Russian Federation. While all the leaderships welcome such proposals in principle, little progress has been made in clarifying the areas or priorities for cooperation, in part because it appears inevitable that in the short term conflicts and disagreements will continue to frustrate practical cooperation. For the most part, such proposals are vague and wide-ranging, the best-publicized being the June 1996 declaration 'For Inter-Ethnic Accord, Peace, and Economic and Cultural Cooperation in the Caucasus' signed by the presidents of all the Caucasian republics (south and north) and of the Russian Federation. The main practical significance of the document lay, however, in the boost it gave to President Yeltsin's election campaign, rather than in the implementation of its ideals. Other projects, such as President Shevardnadze's proposal for a 'Common Caucasian Home', have scarcely progressed beyond the declaratory stage. While Azerbaijan and Georgia see the denial of ethnic separatism and counterbalancing Russian power as key objectives for any such regional cooperation, Armenia has quite a different viewpoint. While all accept that a regional approach to the development of transport infrastructure would be desirable, Tbilisi's and Baku's use of blockades puts even that objective out of reach until progress towards resolving the conflicts can be made.

At sub-state level there have been some small steps towards regional cooperation, for example between the administrations of the three contiguous border regions of Armenia, Azerbaijan and Georgia, or at the level of NGO dialogue, but these initiatives remain few and unambitious. Until now, shared interests and consensus on priorities and implementation, which are essential for effective cooperation, have been lacking among the Caucasian states.

Secessionist republics: Karabagh, South Ossetia and Abkhazia

Compared with those of Yerevan, Baku and Tbilisi, the governments of the unrecognized republics of Karabagh, South Ossetia and Abkhazia have very limited potential to pursue foreign policy initiatives. The goal of international recognition of their independence has not been renounced, yet it has become clear that it is not likely to be achieved. Deprived of normal diplomatic channels to promote their interests, Stepanakert, Tskhinvali and Sukhumi have used the international forums established to negotiate settlements for the Caucasian conflicts to argue their case and seek to counter the diplomacy of Baku and Tbilisi. With such limited access to an international system that is in any case predisposed to uphold the principle of state sovereignty and territorial integrity, it is perhaps inevitable that the secessionists appear isolated on the international stage and are widely viewed as obdurate and unreasonable.

The isolation and weakness of the secessionists in the wider international community should not, however, conceal their continuing success in mobilizing support from important external backers. The Karabagh Armenians' links with Yerevan are firmly entrenched: one Karabagh Armenian, Robert Kocharian, is president of Armenia, and another is minister of the interior and national security. Under Kocharian, Yerevan has come round to Stepanakert's position on the approach to a solution. Sukhumi has maintained its links and support in Moscow, particularly within the Duma, while Tskhinvali keeps up its close connections in North Ossetia. Nor is there anything to suggest that the secessionists' support within the Russian military has diminished. In short, while the secessionists may have only limited international representation and presence, they have been skilful in exploiting those external relationships that are most important to their cause.

Russia

Russia remains the sole external state with the power readily to shape developments in the South Caucasus region. Its military, political and economic presence has allowed Moscow to exert influence on the Caucasian countries' internal development, especially the course of the conflicts and their cease-fires and negotiations. As suggested above, perceptions of Russia have been important considerations in the development of Armenia's, Azerbaijan's and Georgia's international relations. If Russia continues to overshadow the region, however, its power has declined relative to that of other external players, and relative to the increasingly independent and assertive governments in Baku, Tbilisi and, to a lesser extent, Yerevan.[9]

Russia's military decline was exposed in the defeat in the Chechen war, which demonstrated the disastrous state of the armed forces and led to a reappraisal in both Moscow and the Caucasian capitals of the desirability and probable effectiveness of the use of military instruments to pursue interests in the region. This marked a radical change, since until then there had been an assumption of Russian invincibility, bolstered by the ease with which a small Russian detachment had intervened to suppress the Gamsakhurdia insurgency in western Georgia in 1993.

Relative loss of economic position has also been marked. As shown in Chapter 5, Russia's economic importance to the south Caucasian states is in steep decline, as their economies gradually adjust to the breakdown of the interdependent links of the Soviet economic system, as they restore historical economic relations across their borders to the south and west, and as other foreign economic players increase their trade and investments in the region. Blockades imposed in connection with the Abkhazian and Chechen conflicts have contributed to the decline in Russia's trade and general economic significance for the region, but it is the overall weakness of the Russian economy that presents the biggest obstacle to the reversal of Russia's relative decline there.

In political terms also Moscow's stature has been seriously undermined. The lack of clear leadership, the failure of decision-making, the interminable power struggles in Moscow, the declining authority of President Yeltsin, and the marked shift in the balance of power between Moscow and regional governments and other actors have all contributed to this process. Again the Chechen war played an important role in exposing political confusion and incompetence in Moscow. The failure of the integrationist CIS project, in spite of Russia's investment of political energy and influence, has also contributed to the exposure of the loss of leadership. Whereas in the first half of the 1990s Moscow's domination of key positions and of the agenda in the CIS went unchallenged, in the second half of the decade other CIS states, Azerbaijan and Georgia among them, have increasingly used the organization as a vehicle to pursue their own divergent interests and to collaborate to frustrate Russian dominance. Even the less ambitious sub-CIS groupings of the Customs Union (Russia, Belarus, Kazakhstan and Kyrgyzstan) and the Russia–Belarus Union have produced few concrete achievements and offer little to attract potential members in the Caucasus.

Some relative decline in Russia's position in the region was an inevitable consequence of the break-up of the Soviet Union and the opening up of the region to other external players, but the decline has been aggravated by the adoption of inconsistent and contradictory policies that are, moreover, inappropriate for the shrinking resources and capabilities of the Russian state.[10] This reflects difficulty in coming to terms with new realities on the part of both the political leadership and the Russian public. 'Post-imperial' is an apt description of the mentality of many Russians in thinking about their country's role, rights and responsibilities in the post-Soviet space in general, and in particular in the Caucasus, with its deep resonance in Russian history and literature.[11] This mentality is a mixture of regret at loss of power and control, resentment at the ingratitude of the former Soviet republics and at the penetration of foreign competitors, and uncertainty about which direction Russia should take and how to frame policies that will steer the country along that course. The mismatch between perceptions and ambitions on the one hand and resources and capabilities on the other offers, however, only a partial explanation of the problems of Russian policy in the Caucasus. Lack of coordination among multiple players and contradictions among competing sets of interests have also been important.

The numerous protagonists in Russian policy in the Caucasus can be divided into three main sets concerned primarily with foreign policy, military-security policy and foreign economic relations. Each of these sets is, however, further subdivided. The foreign policy set includes the ministry of foreign affairs, the presidential apparatus, and the foreign affairs committee of the Duma. The military-security set includes the ministry of defence, the general staff, the several branches of the armed forces and their local commanders, as well as presidential and parliamentary councils and committees concerned with defence and security. The economic group includes the ministries of foreign economic relations and of fuel and energy, commercial concerns (principally oil and gas, financial and military-industrial businesses) and branches and individuals in government sympathetic to them (for example, the long-standing prime minister Viktor Chernomyrdin was always closely associated with oil and gas interests). In addition there are a number of players who do not fit clearly into any one group, among them regional leaders (notably in the North Caucasus and adjacent regions) and individuals, such as businessman-politician Boris Berezovsky, Moscow Mayor Yuri Luzhkov and general-turned-politician Alexander Lebed, each of whom has played a role in Russia's relations with the South Caucasus. Overall, there is limited coordination either between or within the sets, giving rise to competition, lack of clear division of responsibilities and confusion in the formulation and implementation of policies. Moreover, Caucasus policy is sometimes used as an instrument in the institutional and personal conflicts of Moscow politics, for example between the parliament and the president in 1993.[12]

The diversity of actors engaged in policy towards the Caucasus inevitably complicates defining and prioritizing Russia's interests in the region, which can moreover be subdivided into three geographical clusters of interrelated, yet often contradictory, policy interests:[13] a North Caucasus cluster revolving around the concern to maintain stability and control in this fragile border region;[14] a Transcaucasian cluster connected with Russia's involvement in the unresolved conflicts in Azerbaijan and Georgia, with threats from the south to Russian security (pan-Turkism, Islamic fundamentalism, narcotics, organized crime, migration and hostile foreign penetration), and with relations with Armenia, Azerbaijan and Georgia; and a Caspian cluster centred on Russian interests in the development and export of the Caspian basin's oil and gas – interests which can be further subdivided into the commercial interests of Russian companies eager to participate in and profit from Caspian petroleum development, and the strategic economic interests of Russia as an oil- and gas-exporting country, whose interest lies rather in retarding and controlling the development of the petroleum resources of the competitor Caspian states. Different sets of actors have varying levels of involvement and responsibility for formulating and pursuing policy interests in the three clusters.

Against a backdrop of weak leadership, poor coordination and a post-imperial mentality, these disparate groups of actors and interests have converged, diverged and collided in an unpredictable and occasionally dramatic pattern. In policy towards the states of the South Caucasus two broad tendencies can be identified, the one emphasizing control (to be achieved through political and economic pressure and the use of military levers, if necessary), the other prioritizing stability and therefore tending to support internal stability and state-building in the south Caucasian states and to emphasize the development of normal, voluntary and mutually beneficial bilateral political, economic and security relations.

Among the most blatant contradictions among these actors, interests and tendencies were the direct confrontation between the ministries of foreign affairs and of fuel and energy over how to respond to the 1994 signing of the first major international consortium for the development of Azerbaijan's offshore oil reserves and the sensational revelation in the Duma Defence Committee in spring 1997 of massive secret arms transfers to Armenia.

In attempting to trace and project the development of Russian policy in the Caucasus, it is, therefore, essential to bear in mind that confusion and volatility rather than measured evolution are the hallmarks of the process, and this complicates the effort to sketch a coherent pattern and extrapolate into the future.[15] Nevertheless, phases and trends can be discerned.[16] From the end of 1991 to mid-1992 the foreign ministry, which had hitherto had no involvement in what had been a part of the Soviet Union, gave low priority to the Caucasus, seeing it, like Central Asia, as a burden rather than an asset for the new independent Russian state. Already, however, the military-security actors were deeply involved in the region's conflicts. During the process of the Soviet break-up, they were forced to find responses as their Caucasian bases and equipment came under pressure and sometimes attack from nationalists and paramilitaries. Those responses were largely ad hoc, based on the personal, local and institutional affiliations of the local commanders, as well as reflecting the mentality of the Soviet officer corps and defence bureaucracy. This initial period thus allowed for and even to some extent necessitated a relatively independent, proactive and assertive military-security engagement in the face of a weak diplomatic-political involvement.

From mid-1992 until the end of 1994 Moscow's policy towards the Caucasus became more assertive, partly because of the government's need to respond to ultra-nationalist and communist critics who were making inroads in elections in this period, partly in response to anxieties about foreign penetration and the dangers to Russia of pan-Turkist or Islamist ideas spreading from the south to Russia's Turkic and Muslim peoples. This was the phase in which Moscow formulated a sphere of influence policy towards the 'near abroad', aiming to establish exclusive rights in guarding borders, in mediating conflicts and providing peace-keepers, in economic relations, and in protecting the rights of Russian-speakers. The structural framework to achieve this was intended to be the CIS, but in the face of the persistent failure of CIS integration, bilateral relations, often scarcely voluntary on the part of reluctant 'partners' such as Azerbaijan and Georgia, became the policy's main vehicle.

From the end of 1994 and the start of the Chechen war, a third phase began, with concerns about internal stability in Russia (especially in the North Caucasus), and a growing awareness of the limitations on resources and capabilities, leading to a reassessment of priorities in the South Caucasus and a greater emphasis on supporting regional stability and more cooperative relations with Azerbaijan and Georgia. This trend was supported by the increasingly influential business lobbies that were developing interests in Caspian energy development.

This trend, though scarcely consistent and subject to frequent reversals and contradictions in specific areas, still continues and, even in the face of the current political and economic crises and uncertainty in Russia, appears likely to continue further. Russia's relative decline in the South Caucasus is unlikely to be reversed for many years – at least until Russia is able to reform its economy, rebuild its military and resolve some of its major internal political issues, most importantly the relative balance of power between central and regional government, and between government and non-government (notably commercial) actors. In the meantime, any attempt to project power more forcefully, even among the small weak states of the Caucasus, is likely to overstretch resources and prove counterproductive in relation to more vital interests, especially in the North Caucasus. A rational calculation of the balance of interests and advantage for Russia argues for a policy designed to secure political, security and economic interests through the promotion of regional stability and mutually beneficial relations with the south Caucasian states. The possibility cannot, however, be excluded that either a new, more nationalist government in Moscow or, in the absence of effective leadership, one of the several policy actors with interests in the Caucasus might seek to reassert Russian hegemony, and that this effort, even if ultimately unsuccessful and counterproductive for Russia, could undermine the small states of the region in the process.

Finally, before considering the interests and policies of other regional and extra-regional players in the South Caucasus, it should be borne in mind that Russia's decline in the region is relative to the position of unchallenged domination it enjoyed during the Soviet period. The break-up of the Soviet Union into independent states and the lifting of the artificial restrictions on the south Caucasian countries' international links has led to a significant adjustment of the geopolitical and geo-economic balance. Nearly a decade later, however, Russia retains a far more powerful presence in the region than any other foreign state, none of which, aware of the limitations of their own ability to project power, have sought to challenge its position. Only in the spheres of investment, humanitarian aid, technical support and economic assistance is Russia at an absolute disadvantage.

All other foreign states and international organizations have, therefore, to frame policies that take into account Russia's continuing presence and interests in the region. All, moreover, have to consider the relative priority of their interests in the South Caucasus against their interests in relations with Russia. Policy-makers in Ankara, Tehran, Washington and Brussels have this in common: in their consideration of Caucasus policy, they have to take into account the possible Russian reaction and its impact on bilateral relations with Russia. And since for all of them, relations with Russia and the outcome of political and economic developments in Russia retain primary importance, the Russian dimension is given substantial weight in their considerations. This tendency to formulate Caucasus policy with half an eye on Moscow has been reinforced by departmental tradition, since all foreign states have developed their policy staffs and diplomats for the CIS countries on the basis of old Soviet departments, whose expertise and emphasis were oriented towards Russia and Moscow.

Turkey and Iran

For both Ankara[17] and Tehran[18] the collapse of the Soviet Union removed a major source of threat, created new opportunities, and gave rise to new challenges and problems. This situation, which was completely unexpected, found both governments ill-equipped to formulate and implement policy towards the Caucasus in terms of information, cadres, infrastructure and presence in the region.

Turkey's and Iran's interest in the South Caucasus was reinforced by their long historical associations with the region, which made it appear a natural arena for renewed engagement. For both, however, the post-Soviet situation was fraught with danger as much as pregnant with opportunity. The conflicts and instability in the Caucasus had the potential to destabilize their border regions. Eastern Turkey has for decades been in a state of chronic instability and internal conflict, as Ankara has failed either to satisfy or to suppress Kurdish demands for recognition, cultural rights and self-determination. The effort to suppress those demands has led to a long-running war between the Turkish military and Kurdish guerrillas. Any possibility that guerrillas might find refuge or support in the Caucasus (where there are also Kurdish populations, including in Armenia) poses a serious threat. Armenian irredentism and the contentious issue of the 1915 Genocide present an ideological, if not currently a military or political, challenge to Turkey's territorial integrity and statehood.

Iran's northwestern border provinces are relatively stable, although there have been occasional demonstrations of public discontent there, as in other parts of the country. The population of the northwest is, however, predominantly Azeri. For decades there have been sporadic calls for greater cultural rights for Iran's Azeris, and at the end of the Second World War the Soviet Union briefly supported an independent republic in Iranian Azerbaijan. There has been concern in Tehran about the potential impact on Iranian Azeris of the establishment of an independent Azerbaijani state, and of the calls from Baku (especially from Elchibey and other nationalist politicians) for closer links between or even for the unification of the divided Azeri people. Iran was also threatened with a major refugee crisis (following Armenian victories in 1993–4) and with border violations and even overspill of fighting (in 1990 and 1993–4). National security and regional stability have been key interests of both Turkey and Iran and have led to their support for all initiatives to negotiate peace (thus Iran has supported the OSCE Minsk Group negotiation process on Karabagh, although it is the only country of the region excluded from the organization).

The same interests have encouraged both Turkey and Iran to support the sovereignty and sustainability of the Caucasian states, which they have done through recognition of their independence and territorial integrity, through support for their membership in international organizations and through bilateral treaties and agreements in the political, economic and security fields.

Geopolitical and strategic interests have also influenced policy, with both countries reluctant to antagonize Moscow for the sake of smaller interests in the Caucasus. They have also been concerned not to precipitate too deep a rift in their already tense bilateral relations. Turkey has also exploited its Caucasus policy to reaffirm its importance for Western strategic interests (an importance which was less obvious following the Soviet collapse), by promoting its status as a gateway to the region and by urging greater involvement from international organizations such as the OSCE, the UN and NATO. The formation of the Black Sea Economic Cooperation (BSEC) in 1992 fits this pattern. Iran's primary strategic interest has been in frustrating Washington's policy of containment. Growing Western and US engagement has caused concern to Tehran, which has tried to enmesh Iran with the region through bilateral relations and the promotion of a variety of international organizations linking it with the Caucasian (and Central Asian) states. The expansion of ECO in 1992 to include Afghanistan, the five Central Asian states and Azerbaijan should be seen in this light, as should the so far unrealized initiative launched the same year to establish a Caspian Sea Cooperation Organization.

Economic interests include support for Turkish and Iranian commercial engagement, with both countries keen to develop their export-led manufacturing industry. Turkey's economic development is more advanced than Iran's, but Iran possesses the advantage of geography in developing economic relations with Azerbaijan, the biggest and richest of the south Caucasian markets. The scale of trade and economic relations will be discussed in Chapter 5.

For both Ankara and Tehran the development of transport infrastructure to connect with the South Caucasus has been an important priority. A number of new border crossings have been opened, including a new bridge and direct road link between Iran and Armenia. The inadequacy of the Soviet infrastructure has been aggravated by the blockades that have closed Turkey's best road and only rail links with the region (which passed through Armenia), and Iran's only rail and best road links (which traversed Nakhichevan). For both states, establishing a place in the region's emerging transport and communications network has strategic as well as economic significance, promising to underpin Turkey's importance for the West, and helping to embed Iran in a regional nexus, thereby frustrating Washington's efforts to isolate the Islamic Republic. Securing a role in the transportation of Caspian oil and gas exports has been viewed in both Ankara and Tehran as having special significance in this regard.

In terms of cultural and ideological interests, Turkey views itself as a gateway to the West for the new states, and as a model of a modern, secular, democratic, yet Muslim, country, successfully pursuing a market-oriented economic reform programme and a pro-Western foreign policy. In addition Turkey offered to the Turkic republics (Azerbaijan, Kazakhstan, Kyrgyzstan, Uzbekistan and Turkmenistan) and Turkic peoples of the Russian Federation a pan-Turkic vision of a new brotherhood of Turkic states and peoples stretching from the Mediterranean to China. The cultural ties were particularly strong in relation to Azerbaijan, since language differences are smallest in this case, and because of the Azeri community in Turkey. The success of the Azeri lobby in mobilizing public support has been instrumental in holding Ankara back from establishing normal political and economic relations with Armenia until the Karabagh dispute is resolved. This has run counter to Ankara's strategic and economic interests. Cultural relations have been developed through training and study programmes, encouraging academic and cultural exchange, broadcasting and distributing literature, as well as through a series of Turkic summits, whose achievements were sentimental and rhetorical (though still disturbing for Russia, Iran and Armenia) rather than concrete.

Iran, by contrast, represented a revolutionary Islamic model of cultural and social development, an anti-Western international orientation emphasizing cooperation among developing, particularly Islamic, countries, and a model for economic development that rejected the dominance of the international capitalist system and prioritized the role of state and social actors in achieving economic self-sufficiency and social justice. Tehran also promoted a vision of the Caucasus and Central Asia as part of a millennium-old Persian cultural sphere, whose links could now be resumed after two centuries of Russian-Soviet interruption. Tehran attempted to use similar instruments in developing its cultural relations, though the place of Turkic summits was filled by encouraging the 'Muslim' states of the Caucasus and Central Asia to join and actively participate in the OIC and initiatives to promote Persian language and culture. Iran's Islamic colleges have welcomed students from Azerbaijan to train as clerics for the country's rejuvenated religious establishment. Both Ankara and Tehran have recognized that their cultural interests have little resonance in Armenia and Georgia, that they are in competition, and that both are a source of anxiety to Russia.

Tensions and contradictions between these interests have shaped Ankara's and Tehran's Caucasus policies over the last decade. Between 1988 (when the Soviet system in the Caucasus began to unravel) and 1991, both Ankara and Tehran adopted a hesitant and cautious policy based primarily on maintaining stable relations with Moscow. Neither recognized the independence of the Caucasian republics until Moscow voluntarily let them go.

From late 1991 to 1992 or 1993 they became involved in a brief but exciting competition for supremacy in both Central Asia and the Caucasus. Turkey, with the strong support of Washington, urged the new states to adopt its model for development, while Iran warned against the dire consequences of succumbing to the West's embrace and extolled the virtues of its own model of Islamic development and rejection of great power domination.

Insofar as either Ankara or Tehran gained an advantage in this competition in the South Caucasus, it was Ankara, since the ideals of democracy and secularism and the potential benefits of a pro-Western orientation and market economics were more in harmony with elite and public aspirations in the new states. The pan-Turkist vision also held considerable appeal to many Azeri nationalists, including President Elchibey and other members of the APF government, whereas Iran's insistence on the shared Persian heritage and reminders that Persian was until the nineteenth century the predominant language of culture and government in Azerbaijan (and the medium of expression for cultural heroes such as Nizami Ganjavi) were far from welcome.

Turkey's and Iran's rivalry in the Caucasus and Central Asia was, however, soon revealed to be based on a false premise (though one briefly held not only by Ankara and Tehran, but also by Washington and Moscow). This premise was that the end of the Soviet Union would lead to a complete collapse of Russia's influence in the region and a consequent power vacuum, which in turn would inevitably be filled by a new dominant power. This perception cast the Caucasian states in the role of passive objects of foreign influence, underestimating their capacity to develop their own priorities and choose their own international orientations. More importantly, the prediction of a power vacuum was soon revealed to be false. By the end of 1992 Russian Caucasus policy was already entering the 'sphere of influence' phase described above. This shift was reflected in Azerbaijan in the 1993 coup against Abulfaz Elchibey, and in Heydar Aliyev's subsequent recognition of Russia's continuing importance for Azerbaijan, symbolized by its rejoining the CIS. In Georgia, by the end of 1993, Russian domination seemed complete, as Shevardnadze was forced to accept the curtailment of Georgian sovereignty and complete military dependence on Moscow in order to secure Russian rescue from imminent state collapse. The failure of Turkish, Iranian and international mediation efforts in the region's conflicts, in contrast to Moscow's success in negotiating cease-fires and dominating peace-keeping arrangements, merely reinforced the pattern.

Moreover, other external players, notably the United States, Europe, and international organizations and financial institutions, began to play an increasing role in the South Caucasus. Armenia, Azerbaijan and Georgia had a far more pressing need for mediation, humanitarian assistance, investment and credit than for models, and this also revealed the limitations of Turkish and Iranian economic capabilities.

These developments rendered the vaunted competition between Turkey and Iran more or less irrelevant. In any case, both Yerevan and Ankara had recognized the need to moderate their rivalry in order to maintain bilateral relations. In Turkey the inability to offer effective support to Azerbaijan in the Karabagh war or to the pro-Turkish APF government against the coup in summer 1993, or generally to challenge the restoration of Russia's position, was a bitter and sobering lesson on the limits of Ankara's capabilities. The tenuousness of Turkey's access to Azerbaijan and the Caspian was starkly revealed: the blockade closed routes through Armenia, and internal instability and Russian control of frontiers constrained communications through Georgia.

Since then Turkish policy has been modest in its ambitions, focusing more on commercial interests, on support for international efforts to promote peace and stability, on denying potential support for Kurdish guerrillas, and on promoting Turkey's role in the developing east–west transport corridor, particularly as the route for the main pipeline for oil exports by the AIOC consortium. The development of links with Georgia and the consolidation of close relations with Azerbaijan, which suffered following Elchibey's ouster and have since been marred by a number of frictions, have been important priorities.

Tehran was in the main relieved to be able to withdraw from a competition it could not win and content to see Russia resume its role as guarantor of regional security and stability. Like Ankara, Tehran has adopted increasingly pragmatic policies that are better suited to its resources, with an emphasis on the resolution of conflicts, the promotion of stability, countering any threat to Iran's internal stability emanating from Azeri nationalism, the pursuit of commercial interests, and the development of north–south transport and communications links, including oil and gas pipelines (this is one area where Turkish–Iranian competition remains intense), roads, railways and power grids. Tehran has recognized that its cultural interests have little resonance in any of the Caucasian countries, including 'Muslim' Azerbaijan, where even among the relatively few people who possess a developed sense of Shi'i Muslim identity, it is only a small number (including the Islamic Party) who look to Iran for spiritual and political leadership. Many others, including the state-sponsored clerical establishment, view Iranian Islam with ambivalence at best.[19] Iranian–Azeri relations, though more stable since Aliyev came to power, are still beset by friction and misunderstanding. Relations with Georgia, and particularly Armenia, by contrast have developed relatively smoothly.

The current pragmatic trend in Iranian and Turkish policy is likely to continue and, coupled to the development of transport infrastructure, will lead to a gradual strengthening of their relations with the Caucasian states, but without allowing either to develop a dominant position in any country, let alone in the region as whole. The trend could be interrupted by the adoption of policies by Yerevan or Baku that threatened the sovereignty and integrity of Turkey and Iran respectively. Even this, however, or the resumption of fighting in the unresolved conflicts or renewed political chaos in one of the Caucasian states would be unlikely to draw an interventionist policy from governments in Ankara and Tehran whose main interests and energies are absorbed at home and in other international directions. Conversely, the more likely scenarios of the lifting of blockades and the withdrawal of Russian border guards would give a substantial boost to Turkey and Iran's engagement in the region.

Extra-regional actors: The United States and Europe
While many states have established relations with Armenia, Azerbaijan and Georgia, and a few, among them Israel and Japan, have developed significant specific interests in the region, the United States and Europe remain the only major extra-regional players in the South Caucasus.

Western policy towards the South Caucasus has been characterized by the same complexities and contradictions between various sets of interests as that of other international actors. In Armenia, Azerbaijan and Georgia themselves those interests are few and mostly mutually compatible, and there is, moreover, no real disagreement between the US and European conception of these interests.[20]

The region is perceived as possessing significance for the West in terms of its strategic location at Europe's southeastern periphery, bordering Russia and the Black Sea to the north and west, NATO member Turkey to the west, the Middle East, the Islamic world and Iran to the south and east, and the Caspian Sea and Central Asia to the east. This pivotal location makes it important for the West to promote peace, security and stability in the South Caucasus and to discourage the domination of any regional power or the penetration of anti-Western ideology.

The other significant Western interest in the South Caucasus stems from the petroleum resources of the Caspian basin, the West's commercial interests engaged in their development, and its energy security interests in their export to European markets via routes that cannot be interdicted by potentially hostile states or disrupted by instability and conflict. The importance of the energy factor has been growing steadily since the end of 1994, when the AIOC contract was signed and the first major commitment of Western investment in Azerbaijan was made. As commercial interests have become more extensively involved in Caspian petroleum development, so the need for regional stability and for the exclusion of external domination has become increasingly important for Western companies and governments anxious to ensure that the oil can be safely exported. The West sees its strategic and economic interests as complementing each other and harmonizing with the interests of the Caucasian states.

American and European policy-makers have also achieved broad consensus that the best way to secure these interests is by supporting the independence of the Caucasian countries, helping to bring about sustainable peaceful resolutions to their conflicts, promoting political, economic and military reform, and encouraging the region's integration into the international community, particularly European and Euro-Atlantic structures. Energy and pipeline development, it is argued, should be a positive-sum game in which all can benefit from some share in the region's petroleum wealth. If these objectives can be achieved the region will be made secure from internal and external threats, and will become a friendly environment for the operations of Western businesses. Both the United States and Europe (individual states and the European Union) have invested considerable sums in humanitarian aid, in technical assistance for the development of market economies and of democracy, civil society and human rights, and in credits to support government budgets. A large part of this investment has been channelled through IFIs, international organizations and NGOs. Western states also supported and participated in international (UN and OSCE) mediation of the Caucasian conflicts, and have used NATO's PfP to encourage military reform.

Inevitably there have been inconsistencies – the promotion of democracy and human rights has clashed with support for the sovereignty and stability of countries whose regimes show scant regard for these ideals; participation in Azerbaijan's oil development may be seen to prejudice neutrality in mediating the Karabagh conflict – but the principal contradictions and problems in Western policy towards the Caucasus do not stem from the incompatibility of interests in the region itself, but rather from the complex meshing of interests and policies in the Caucasus with other sets of interests and policies. This is particularly true of the United States.

Like Iran and Turkey, the West at times finds its Caucasus policy a hostage to its Russia policy. From the time of Gorbachev onwards, Western policy-makers have consistently identified supporting the 'reformers' in power in Moscow as a key objective. They have been reluctant, therefore, to adopt policies which might weaken the position of President Yeltsin and his governments in their power struggle with the opposition. At times this objective has been in harmony with Caucasus policy – it has been argued that Russia's reformers share with the West an interest in preventing Russian military domination in the Caucasus, which would in turn be deleterious for political and military reform in Russia – but often Caucasus policy has had to make way for Russia policy. Critics accuse the West of making too many concessions to Russian demands and failing to prioritize its own interests in the region, and those of the Caucasian states whose independence it is committed to support.[21] The 1996 negotiations over the flank limits of the CFE Treaty saw the West ignore Azerbaijan's objections to proposed treaty revisions for the sake of reaching agreement with Russia.

Antagonistic relations between the United States and Iran have also had an impact. Again, Caucasian policy interests have had to give way to other priorities. The objectives of promoting positive-sum outcomes in Caspian energy development and of encouraging the Caucasian states to diversify their international economic relations to reduce dependence on Russia clash with the policy of isolating and containing Iran, one possible avenue for such diversification. In 1995 President Clinton personally intervened with President Aliyev to eject the National Iranian Oil Company from an Azerbaijani oil consortium in which US companies had a stake. Even in 1998, when US–Iranian relations had thawed a little, senior State Department and Department of Commerce officials were excluding plans for pipelines through Iran as 'totally unacceptable'.[22] Apart from exposing the contradictions and relative priorities in US policy, such statements cause disquiet in Europe (which has a long-running argument with Washington over Iran policy), frustrate the interests of US companies in the Caspian, and give substance to Russian and Iranian accusations of US arrogance. Washington's strong advocacy of Turkey's regional role and its pipeline project can also be attributed as much to the desire to promote Turkey as a strategic ally and to reward Ankara for its rapprochement with Israel as to US interests in the Caucasus.

US policy and, to a lesser extent, the policies of some European countries have also been influenced by the lobbying of interest groups. The US Armenian lobby has succeeded in securing a very high level of financial support for Armenia, while constraining the administration's freedom to offer assistance to the Azerbaijani government. Indirectly, through its influence on Iran policy, the Jewish American lobby also has an impact. Oil interests in the United States, the UK and other Western countries have urged that high priority should be given to Azerbaijan and to Caspian issues.

If Europe's policy reveals fewer contradictions than that of Washington, European states, both individually and collectively, have been less proactive and effective in formulating, expressing and pursuing Western interests. Although the Caucasus is an area where there are few rivalries between European states, still it has proved difficult to achieve a common European policy or approach. The EU is a very significant donor of humanitarian and technical assistance to the Caucasus, and has been a vigorous advocate of new transport and communications projects, while European companies figure prominently in trade and investment. Yet Europe has not developed a political agenda for the region and remains an unassertive player. Both in Europe and in the United States it has been difficult to achieve a consistent application of attention, effort and resources to secure Caucasian policy objectives. Growing commercial interests are making that goal appear more attainable, and in the last two years Washington in particular has given increasing emphasis to the region's strategic importance for the West. Whether this declared emphasis will find expression in a realignment of priorities between Caucasian and other sets of policies remains to be seen. Even with a relatively uncoordinated and sometimes contradictory Caucasus policy, the West's relative position is likely to continue to improve, since the Caucasian states all welcome Western engagement, while only the West is in a position to provide essential investment and credits.

Summing up

The international relations of the South Caucasus are characterized by a high level of volatility and complexity. Armenia, Azerbaijan and Georgia are small weak states, vulnerable to assertive foreign policies by neighbouring powers. Moreover, the complex international dimensions of the region's conflicts, and of its ethnic and religious composition, exacerbate that vulnerability.

Russia, Turkey, Iran and the West all identify the region as having strategic importance for their interests, while subordinating Caucasus policy to other priorities. The policies of all towards the Caucasian states are inconsistent and sometimes contradictory.

Russia remains the strongest external power in the South Caucasus and the only one that currently has the potential to assert its hegemony over the region, but its relative position is in a decline that has been exacerbated by the contradictions and incoherence of its policies. Turkey, Iran and the West are all experiencing a relative enhancement of their position, and all those major actors appear strong relative to the Caucasian states.

Notwithstanding their weakness, the geopolitical balance is currently benign for the Caucasian states. No external power is at present in a position to dominate the region without excessive costs. All tend publicly to identify their interests with regional stability and cooperative relations, rather than with control and a zero-sum strategy. Nevertheless, international rivalry persists beneath the surface, with Washington adopting a zero-sum approach to Iranian engagement in the region, vigorously promoting a Turkish route for the main Caspian pipeline and actively bidding for influence in Georgia, where Russia has important security interests at stake. The current equilibrium may, therefore, be short-lived, and could be replaced by a new international configuration allowing the Caucasian states fewer choices and less room for manoeuvre.

Chapter 5

Economy

Since independence, Armenia, Azerbaijan and Georgia have faced exceptionally difficult circumstances for economic development. A number of the problems are shared with all other 'transition' economies and are connected with the attempt to change the basis of economic organization from a command system to a market system. Others are shared with the other non-Russian post-Soviet republics, whose twentieth-century economic development within the USSR left them particularly ill-equipped to reconstitute themselves as national economies.

Other difficulties are particular to the Caucasus, stemming from the conflicts and blockades, and from the peculiar characteristics of state-building and political development in the three countries (see Chapters 2 and 3). Armenia, in addition, is still struggling with the economic and social legacy of a massive earthquake that occurred in December 1988. The region's physical geography, climate and natural resources also, of course, shape economic development.

In other respects, the Caucasian countries resemble other small states. Small national markets oblige them to look outward for purchasers for their products and for investment. Important for all three states is the question of regional cooperation, which has the potential markedly to increase their competitiveness and attraction to investors. But regional cooperation has not only economic but also political, security and international aspects, which greatly complicate progress. More generally, international interests in the region, both strategic and commercial, exert a strong influence on Caucasian economic development. Azerbaijan, as a potentially significant producer and exporter of oil and gas, is particularly exposed to these external influences, and in this respect bears comparison with other oil-producing states.

Dense interlinkage of issues at different levels and across different fields is a characteristic of the region's development. Another important and related characteristic is the continuing volatile flux of political, social, cultural and international developments in the region, all of which can have a strong and unpredictable impact on economic matters.

The Soviet and post-Soviet context

Soviet government produced rapid economic development in the three south Caucasian republics.[1] Over the whole Soviet period Armenia, Azerbaijan and Georgia experienced high GDP growth, though rates dropped off sharply in the 1980s. They were transformed from predominantly rural societies with an agricultural economic base, to mainly urban societies the majority of whose population worked in the industrial and service sectors. Nevertheless, even at the end of the Soviet period the Caucasian republics lagged behind most other Soviet republics (though they outstripped Central Asia) on most economic indices. The principal characteristics of Soviet economic policy were a heavy emphasis on industrial development, with relatively low priority for the service sector; a high degree of Union-wide specialization, leading to deep inter-dependence among republics for inputs and markets; a command system that ignored market mechanisms, and directed development by setting targets for output and by investment flows from the centre; and the sub-ordination of local and republican interests to the interests of the centre and the Union as a whole. Shortage and a variety of compensatory redistributive mechanisms (party privilege, corruption, the black market, informal economic networks based on kinship, locality, Communist Party membership, etc.) were universal characteristics of the Soviet economy.

These characteristics combined with the natural resources of the region to produce a distinctive pattern of development. Azerbaijan possessed a large oil and gas industry and associated machinery and petrochemicals industries. Georgia's and Armenia's industrial development was more diverse, with the latter having a relatively advanced light industrial base, in part thanks to the Armenian party leadership's successful lobbying in Moscow. By international standards, however, Soviet industrial plant and technology were mostly obsolete. Agriculture and food industries were important in all three republics, most so in Georgia and least in Armenia. The tourist industry was an important source of earnings and employment for Georgia. One characteristic of the region's economic development, though exaggerated in Soviet popular myth, was the relative strength of private, informal enterprise, much of which was criminalized by the statist Soviet ideology.

All three were heavily dependent on trade with other Soviet republics (Russia alone accounted for over 50 per cent of trade). By contrast, the development of economic relations with non-Soviet partners was severely stunted, and trade among the three south Caucasian republics was also relatively poorly developed. Armenia had the highest level of trade dependence of any Soviet republic. Imports of inputs for industry, of consumer goods and of foodstuffs (grain, meat and dairy products) were vital for all three. Armenia and Georgia were also large net importers of energy. The products of their heavy and light industries and their agriculture were marketable only in other Soviet republics.

Human development in the Soviet period also achieved significant progress, particularly in education and health care. Living standards improved dramatically, particularly if one makes comparisons with the pre-Soviet period, or with neighbouring Middle Eastern societies. In general, however, in this respect also the region as a whole and Azerbaijan in particular remained below all-Union averages.

After 1991, the Soviet economic system rapidly collapsed. Investment and budget flows from the centre were reduced and then stopped. Soviet industries, which had not been developed to compete on market terms, were unable to survive the combined shocks of external competition for markets and the rapid escalation towards world levels of costs for inputs, energy and transport. Excessive specialization and trade interdependence with remote post-Soviet republics proved serious handicaps, particularly when the transport of goods and energy became subject to interruptions because of wars, blockades and virtual state collapse. The breakdown of regional trade and payments agreements with other post-Soviet states and of the rouble zone in 1993 gave additional shocks.

Soviet bureaucratic and management traditions left government, industry and agriculture ill-equipped to cope with the new conditions. Formulating and implementing economic policy for an independent country operating in a competitive international system calls for very different skills from those possessed by Soviet bureaucrats and party officials, whose career advancement depended largely on correct responses to various prompts from the centre. A Soviet manager's experience in negotiating output targets, securing supplies of scarce inputs and providing for the social needs of employees gave little preparation for tackling the issues of investment, cashflow, productivity and marketing that confront a modern business manager.

The Caucasian tradition of private enterprise developed in the Soviet shadow economy ensured that the market mentality was relatively developed in some cases, and has doubtless contributed to recovery in the small-scale retail, farming and consumer production sectors. It has also, however, contributed to the continuing strength of the shadow[2] and criminal sectors in the Caucasian economies.

Certain specific features of political development in the Caucasus have an economic dimension. The political economy was discussed in Chapter 2; in summary, the concentration of power in the hands of a few scarcely accountable presidents and ministers provides favourable conditions for persistent crypto-statism, patronage, monopolies and corruption.[3] Wars and blockades multiply the opportunities for contraband trade, and for military and security structures to seize and retain control of certain economic activities. The corruption or mismanagement of privatization has encouraged asset-stripping, which has accelerated the inevitable deterioration of infrastructure and plant with the passage of time and the failure of investment.

The post-Soviet period has, however, also provided powerful positive stimuli for economic development. Market reforms and access to international markets provide the basis for new industries to emerge. International credits and assistance have supported government budgets, social welfare and the reform process. Foreign investment in various sectors and in transport infrastructure is helping to establish or re-establish internationally competitive industries.

Macroeconomic development

In all three countries post-Soviet governments have adopted policies aimed at transforming the economy to a market basis and integrating into the world system. Political opponents and critics have argued that the governments in fact pay only lip-service to these policies in order to ingratiate themselves with the West and the IFIs on whose support they depend. Certainly there have been differences in the level of commitment to market reform shown by Armenian, Azerbaijani and Georgian governments. Armenia's economic policy was from the early independence period in the hands of committed liberal economic reformers, while internal political stability provided a more favourable backdrop than the turmoil in Azerbaijan and Georgia. In most areas of economic policy

Yerevan introduced reforms earlier than Tbilisi or Baku. In Azerbaijan efforts to implement a thoroughgoing economic reform programme began only in 1995, while Georgia, though it could not initiate serious reforms until it restored basic law and order in 1994–5, has been an enthusiastic proponent of liberalizing reform since then.

The debate over economic policy has not been one-sided, and left-wing political parties – which are a force to be reckoned with in all three states – continue to advocate a socialist or a mixed system with a strong emphasis on social priorities. The limited poll evidence suggests that there is significant popular support for such models.[4] More effective opposition to liberalizing economic policies has come from those with vested interests in the preservation of the old system and its subsidies. Industrial managers and ministry bureaucrats alike have tended to see the risks of reform as outweighing the opportunities it presents and have done what they can to slow the pace of reform. In all three states the ministries and structures responsible for the implementation of economic reform have in any case lacked the political power and support to challenge the even more powerful vested interests in the current intermediate system of political economy. These interests are often 'untouchable' and effectively above the law, including as they do presidents, cabinet ministers and the heads of other state structures, among them armies and police forces. In Armenia, for instance, active government promotion of economic reform has waxed and waned in inverse relation to the demands of the Karabagh war and the priority given to the interests of the 'power' ministries of defence and the interior.

Gross domestic product
The negative consequences of the collapse of the Soviet system, coupled with factors specific to the region, resulted in catastrophic economic declines (see Figure 1). In 1992 Armenia's GDP dropped by 52 per cent, the steepest annual rate of decline recorded for any post-Soviet state, while in 1994 Georgia's GDP was only 23 per cent of its 1989 level, the deepest recession recorded for any post-Soviet state. In 1997, after several years of recovery, the combined GDPs of Armenia, Azerbaijan and Georgia were still only 40 per cent of the 1988 level.[5] The years 1993–5 marked the bottom of the recession. The return to positive growth was connected with the cease-fires negotiated in the Karabagh, South Ossetian and Abkhazian conflicts, the restoration of law and order in Georgia, and the adoption of stringent macroeconomic stabilization programmes supported by IMF Systemic Transformation Facilities and

Economy

Figure 1: Real GDP

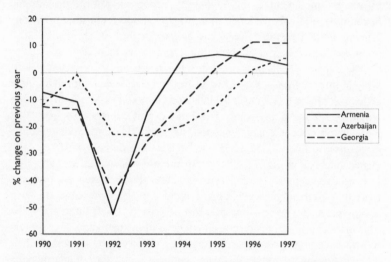

Sources: *Armenia Economic Trends; Georgian Economic Trends; Azerbaijan Economic Trends*; EBRD, *Transition Report Update* (April 1997).
Note on data: Economic statistics for the three Caucasian states are deficient and unreliable. The extensive shadow economy goes unrecorded and there are problems of methodological accuracy. In addition there have been numerous changes in the Soviet and post-Soviet systems for the collection and calculation of statistics, while there are also national differences between the three states. The data used in the figures are drawn from several sources, principally the IMF, World Bank, EBRD, CIS Statistical Committee and Armenian, Azerbaijani and Georgian government sources; this diversity of sources introduces further inconsistencies. All statistics and charts are, therefore, broadly indicative rather than precisely accurate.

World Bank Rehabilitation Credits. In 1994 Armenia was among the first post-Soviet states to record positive growth; Georgia followed in 1995 and Azerbaijan in 1996.

Sustaining recovery, even from such a low base, has presented problems in Armenia, where a combination of continuing economic blockade and failure to implement reforms which clashed with powerful vested interests led to faltering growth rates in 1996 and 1997, though the first two quarters of 1998 showed a recovery to year-on-year growth rates of over 6 per cent.[6] The prospects for Georgia and Azerbaijan appear brighter, with Georgian annual growth rates standing at over 11 per cent in 1996 and 1997 and predicted to remain strong.[7] Azerbaijan's growth rates have gradually accelerated since 1995, with the first two quarters of 1998

124

showing respective increases of 8.2 and 9.9 per cent on the previous year.[8] The gathering flow of direct investment underpins future growth for many years to come.

Budgets

Controlling state budgets has been an important element in stabilization programmes. All states have seen expenditure fall from mid-1990s peaks of around 50 per cent of GDP (at the height of the Karabagh war Armenia's expenditure peaked at an extraordinary 85 per cent of GDP) to below 20 per cent (see Figure 2). Revenue has also declined as a percentage of GDP, but less steeply, so that budget deficits had shrunk, by 1997, to less than 5 per cent of GDP. The cease-fires in the region's wars allowed a reduction in military expenditure, but the greatest savings have been achieved by reducing the number of state employees and cutting social provision and subsidies to enterprises. In Georgia total central and local government employment declined by about 40 per cent, from over 600,000 persons at the beginning of 1995 to around 360,000 at the end of 1996.[9] While the reduction of deficits has been impressive, the social costs have been considerable (see below). The low levels of state employees' wages are, moreover, an important contributing factor to the

Figure 2: Budgets

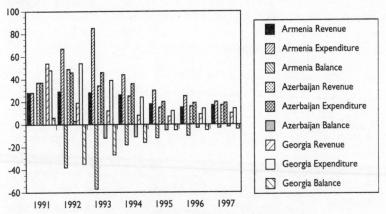

Sources: 1991–6: A.N. Illarionov, 'Regional Growth and Integration in the Transcaucasus', in S.M. Antounian (ed.), *The Transcaucasus Today: Prospects for Regional Integration*, 23–25 June 1997, Edited Conference Report (Yerevan: American University of Armenia, no date), pp. 92–7; 1997: *Armenia Economic Trends; Azerbaijan Economic Trends;* UN/ECE, *Economic Survey of Europe*, 1998, No. 1.

prevalence and seriousness of corruption in the three Caucasian countries.

Foreign grants were an important element in the budgets of Armenia and Georgia in the mid-1990s, but declined to between 1 and 2 per cent of GDP by 1996.[10] Oil royalties, taxes and the contract signature bonuses paid by international consortia are already playing an important role in Azerbaijan's state revenues, accounting for 27, 24 and 31 per cent of state revenues in 1995, 1996 and 1997 respectively.[11]

The level of tax revenue, if comparable to some other CIS countries, remains very low by global standards, and threatens sustainable progress towards balanced budgets. Governments, prompted by IFIs, have given high priority to reforming their tax systems in recent years, and early indications suggest that this is leading to improvements. Nevertheless, lack of transparency, arbitrariness, corruption and absence of trust between tax collectors and taxpayers present persistent obstacles to effective tax regimes in all three states. Georgia's performance is particularly poor in this regard, with tax revenues under 10 per cent of GDP in every year from 1992 to 1997.

Monetary policy and inflation

In 1994 the Caucasian economies scored the highest inflation rates ever recorded in the CIS (see Figure 3). Georgia's annual rate of increase in the consumer price index peaked at over 22,000 per cent, with Armenia's at almost 5,000 per cent and Azerbaijan's at a little over 1,500 per cent. Deregulation of prices, scarcity exacerbated by war and blockade, and

Figure 3: Inflation (consumer prices)

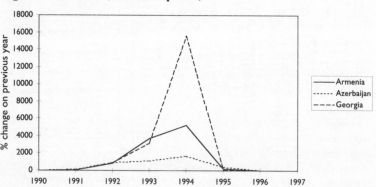

Sources: *Armenia Economic Trends; Azerbaijan Economic Trends; Georgian Economic Trends;* EBRD, *Transition Report Update* (April 1997).

lax control of money supply all contributed to the phenomenon. The subsequent recovery, attributable to peace, greater political stability, economic reform and strict monetary controls, has been scarcely less dramatic, with single-digit inflation in Azerbaijan and Georgia in 1997.

The establishment of national banks and the introduction of national currencies were important steps in allowing Yerevan, Baku and Tbilisi to take control of and stabilize their national economies. Azerbaijan issued its national currency, the manat, as early as 1992 (as much to symbolize national sovereignty as for economic motives), but the Russian rouble continued in parallel use until the beginning of 1994. Georgia started down the road to monetary independence later (April 1993), but its interim coupon soon became sole legal tender (August 1993). In autumn 1995 a new currency, the lari (worth 1 million coupons), was introduced. Armenia adopted its national currency, the dram, only when forced to do so by Russia's refusal in late 1993 to issue further roubles on acceptable terms. Since their introduction, all three currencies have appreciated in real terms against the dollar. Azerbaijan's manat, strengthened by the country's oil potential, has appreciated ten times more than the dram and the lari and by over 500 per cent in real terms.[12]

The banking sector in all three countries remains weak, though there have been important reforms and there are signs that the sector is strengthening. The national banks, supported by IFI technical assistance, have played an important role in achieving exchange rate and price stability, and are now increasingly effective in regulating and supervising the banking sector. All three states have passed legislation intended to bring their banking sectors into line with international standards. In all three countries the tightening of national bank credit and of regulations has led to the closure of many of the small banks that opened in the early 1990s. High, if falling, interest rates and a high proportion of non-performing loans continue to retard development in the sector. The latter problem has made banks wary of lending to enterprises. A number of initiatives have been launched to improve collection of outstanding loans and to write off bad debt, as well as to help encourage credit in the Georgian and Armenian economies – notably American Armenian billionaire Kirk Kirkorian's interest-free loan of US$100 million for credit for small businesses in Armenia.[13]

In Armenia, Azerbaijan and Georgia the commercial banking sector is dominated by a few relatively large banks, which (except in Azerbaijan) comprise the privatized successors to former Soviet savings or sectional banks, as well as the foreign joint venture Midland Bank of Armenia (which opened in March 1996 with a statutory capital of US$4 million, amounting to 33 per cent of the total statutory capital of commercial banks in Armenia). In banking sector reform, as in other areas, Azerbaijan lagged behind Armenia and Georgia; but the strength of investment and oil sector growth is likely to promote relatively dynamic banking sector development in the coming years.

Production

The plummeting GDPs of the early and mid-1990s marked the complete breakdown of the system of production of the old Soviet regime. Already in the perestroika period legislation had been passed to allow private enterprise greater freedom and opportunity. Since independence policy initiatives to regenerate production have centred on privatization and the creation of a new legislative framework that will meet international normative standards for property protection and the regulation of commercial and economic activities. All three governments have received encouragement and large-scale technical assistance in this from Western states and IFIs. The pattern has been uneven, however, with Azerbaijan embarking on serious reform considerably later than Armenia and Georgia.

Privatization

Privatization has been a central plank of the reform platform in all three states. Small, medium and large enterprises are being privatized in sequence. Under a variety of different schemes, shares and vouchers have been distributed to employees and citizens at large, while management buy-outs, auctions and tenders have also been used. In spite of some effort to promote (or portray) a stakeholder mentality, privatization remains controversial and, on the basis of limited survey data, unpopular – though less so in Georgia. Lack of transparency and of stock markets has made it impossible for most potential domestic investors (let alone foreigners and ordinary citizens) to make sound investment decisions. In general public perception, and to a great extent in reality, corruption, insider deals and patronage have allowed a small elite to secure most of the benefits of privatization. Ruthless asset-stripping by the new owners of privatized enterprises has further damaged the public perception of privatization in particular and market economics in general. In the Soviet period many citizens felt genuine pride in their country's industrial achievement, which has made it harder to accept that a high proportion of enterprises are actually unviable and worthless except as scrap under market conditions.[14] Even potentially viable privatized industries have often been unable to develop that potential in the prevailing unfavourable investment, credit, infrastructure and marketing conditions.[15]

Structural reforms, including price liberalization (almost complete in all three states) and a firmer framework of property law, contract law, company law and bankruptcy law, and tighter regulation of accounting, competition and protection for foreign investors, are continuing in all three states. Though it is early to judge their effectiveness, it is likely that these reforms, if momentum is continued and legislation enforced, will make the Caucasian states far more attractive places to invest. The first indications of this may be observed in individual stories of business success, and in the recent upturn in investment in Georgia, but in general the Caucasian countries are still perceived as difficult places to do business, with structural weakness, high political risk and rampant corruption.

Armenia was the first post-Soviet state to privatize land, largely in 1991–2, with 87 per cent of agricultural land in private hands by summer 1997. Housing, much of which was privately owned in the Soviet period, was 80 per cent in private ownership by 1997. The privatization of small enterprises began in 1993 and was virtually complete by 1997, when nearly 90 per cent of medium and large enterprises were also in private hands. In 1997–8, after protracted negotiations over the sale of a number of high-profile large enterprises, among them the telecommunications company and the cognac factory, there was public outcry at the low prices realized for these national assets. By the end of the 1998–9 privatization programme the private-sector share of GDP is expected to be 75 per cent, while in 1997 non-public enterprises already accounted for 70 per cent.[16]

Georgia launched its privatization programme in 1993, and by autumn 1996 nearly 90 per cent of small enterprises had been privatized, as well as most housing (of which a large proportion was already in private hands during the Soviet period). In 1997 new privatization legislation was passed to speed up the process, with 'zero price' auctions for enterprises that remained unsold at cash auctions. By spring 1998 more than 75 per cent of medium and large enterprises had been privatized. In 1997 the private sector generated about 55 per cent of GDP. Georgia allows foreign ownership, and about 20 per cent of the equity in privatized medium and large enterprises has been bought by foreigners. On the basis of government figures, Georgia has been more successful than Armenia or Azerbaijan in creating a stakeholder society, with half a million Georgians reported to be shareholders in privatized enterprises. Legislation on land privatization was passed in March 1996, and two years later more than a quarter of agricultural land was in private hands.[17]

In Azerbaijan, in spite of some tentative moves towards privatization in the early 1990s, the Karabagh war and the political upheavals in Baku in 1992–4 precluded any effective progress. Only in 1996, and under pressure from the IMF, did privatization begin in earnest. By mid-1998 small-scale privatization was virtually complete, with over 18,000 small enterprises sold, but medium/large-scale privatization was still at an early stage. In 1997 the private sector accounted for some 30 per cent of GDP.[18] The transfer of land and housing to private ownership is also in its early stages, though informal privatization through lease arrangements is advanced.

Sectoral developments
In the immediate post-Soviet period output in all sectors declined dramatically, but the decline was uneven, with certain industries dying out altogether. The opening of traditional Soviet markets to international competition, loss of inputs through closure of routes, breakdown of inter-republican trade, exposure to world prices for inputs and transport, and energy shortages (most acute in Armenia in 1992–3) resulted in the complete collapse of certain branches of industry (for example heavy industry in Azerbaijan and light industry in Armenia), but also even for certain branches of agriculture: the production of tea and citrus fruits in Georgia, viticulture in all three countries, and cotton in Azerbaijan. Nevertheless, on the whole industry was the worst-hit sector, so that the share of agriculture in GDP increased significantly. This trend was most

Figure 4: Armenia – sectoral production

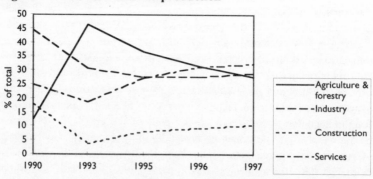

Source: *Armenia Economic Trends* (April–June 1998).

marked in Armenia, where agriculture generated just 13 per cent of GNP in 1990, but 46 per cent in 1993 (see Figure 4).

The incipient recovery has also been unevenly distributed among sectors. Domestic demand, structural reform, energy efficiency and the availability of inputs have favoured the recovery of certain sectors. The fact that shadow economic activity is concentrated in the growth areas suggests that statistics tend to downplay the differential between growing and failing branches.[19]

In Armenia recovery began in the agricultural sector, partly thanks to early privatization, but also as a consequence of the spontaneous relocation of labour to agriculture at the time of the virtual shut-down of industry during the 1992–3 energy crisis. Agricultural recovery has not proved robust, however, with shortages of inputs (fertilizer, water, fuel for machinery), credit and marketing effectively capping the rate of growth. Continuing structural reforms and the development of infrastructure can be predicted to allow a return to stronger growth in the agricultural sector.

Agriculture employs more people than any other sector in all three countries: figures for 1996 were 32 per cent of the gainfully occupied population in Azerbaijan, 41 per cent in Armenia and 52 per cent in Georgia. In Georgia (and in Armenia until 1996) agriculture also contributes more to GDP than any other sector. In all three countries agricultural development has seen a shift away from the export-oriented crops favoured in the Soviet period towards grain and food production for the domestic market.[20]

Growth in energy production was a vital motor for Armenia's recovery, since the recession had been precipitated by the shutting of traditional energy imports via Azerbaijan. Energy's share of industrial production has risen from 3.4 per cent in the trough of recession in 1993 to 27.1 per cent in 1997; the controversial reopening of the Metsamor nuclear power station in autumn 1995 played a crucial role in this recovery. Energy, together with the food and consumer goods industries, is largely responsible for recovery in the industrial sector, whereas Armenia's traditional industrial base only began to show real signs of recovery at the start of 1998. Services – particularly trade – and construction, however, have been the most important growth areas in the Armenian economy.

In Georgia too, agriculture, trade and construction have led the recovery of output. Georgian agriculture's recovery did not begin until 1996, but has so far been more sustained than Armenia's. Industrial performance has been patchy, with recovery concentrated in the energy and food-processing industries, while the branches that constituted the strength of Georgian industry in the Soviet period – metallurgy, machine-building, textiles, etc. – continue to decline.

Azerbaijan's recovery did not begin until 1996. The petroleum sector will be discussed in the following section, but it should be noted here that while it has not directly contributed to recovery – production of oil and gas has continued to fall, if less steeply than in any other branch of industry except electricity generation – it has had a very significant role in stimulating the recovery in the services and construction sectors, which have largely been financed by oil-related foreign direct investment. Services and construction account for about half of GDP and have been responsible for the recovery of output. Agricultural production has stabilized at around 50 per cent of 1990 levels, but has not yet shown sustained growth, partly because Azerbaijan's structural reform of the sector occurred relatively recently.

Energy production has been an important element in the recovery of all three states, though for rather different reasons. Armenia was obliged to give energy development the highest priority, since its traditional import routes had been closed by blockade, leaving the country without power for industrial or domestic purposes for much of 1992–3. Routes through Georgia are now more reliable than in the first half of the decade, but Yerevan hopes to avoid a return to dependence on energy imports, particularly as it now has to pay world prices for gas from Russia and Turkmenistan. It has even been able to export electricity to Georgia. The government is, however, under pressure from the international community and the IFIs to close the Metsamor nuclear power station, which many consider unsafe, and which Yerevan agreed to close in a deal for EBRD support for developing hydroelectric capacity.

Georgia was also heavily dependent on energy imports and amassed a large external debt for natural gas supplies in the early 1990s. This experience led to a priority on improving energy efficiency and domestic energy production. This involved major structural reform of the sector, investment in infrastructure (which had suffered from wars and neglect) and development of generating capacity. Georgia's small-scale oil and gas resources are also a priority for development, with several foreign companies already involved, again primarily in order to substitute energy imports.[21]

Although Azerbaijan was always a net energy exporter and had in 1980 exported about 20 per cent of gas production, it was importing natural gas (mostly from Turkmenistan) to cover nearly half of domestic needs in the 1990s. With the rapid increase in the price of gas imports, the government decided to substitute domestic energy resources, particularly

Figure 5: Azerbaijan – sectoral production

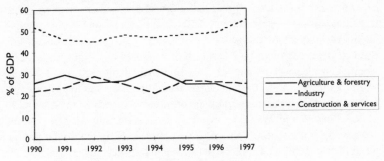

Source: *Azerbaijan Economic Trends* (April–June 1998).

natural gas. Energy policy-making and implementation remain weak, as does structural reform in the energy sector, and gas production has continued to decline. The decision to cease gas imports has resulted in the loss of gas supplies to most of the country, rather than a recovery of gas production, which is expected to occur in parallel with new oil production capacity coming on stream.[22]

The stability suggested by the curves in Figure 5 conceals major shifts in the importance of different branches within each sector. Manufacture in Azerbaijan has been devastated, declining by 88 per cent between 1990 and 1997, but overall industrial production has maintained its share in a declining GDP through the relatively strong performance of the electricity and petroleum branches (see Figure 6).

Figure 6: Azerbaijan – real value production index (1990 = 100)

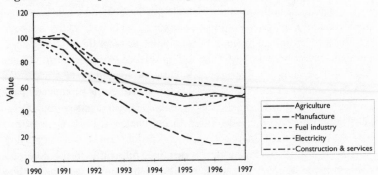

Source: *Azerbaijan Economic Trends* (April–June 1998).

Oil

The oil resources in the Caspian Sea offshore from Azerbaijan represent the single world-class economic asset of the Caucasian region. Azerbaijan's oil industry dates back over a hundred years and at the turn of the century Baku accounted for nearly half of world crude oil production. Azerbaijan claims both the world's first drilled oil well and the first offshore oil well. Until the Soviet period the industry was mainly owned and managed by Russians and other foreigners. Already in the aftermath of the First World War and the Russian Revolution, foreign powers competed for access to or control over Caspian oil. In the Soviet period the industry developed rapidly, with production peaking in 1941 at 24 million tonnes per year (mt/y), or 70 per cent of Soviet production. Baku was one objective of the Nazi invasion of the Soviet Union. Awareness of this dependence, as well as the depletion of existing onshore and shallow offshore fields and Soviet technical constraints on deep-water extraction, led to a shift in priorities for the Soviet oil industry, with Azerbaijan's production falling off in the postwar period, as western Siberia took the lion's share of investment and became the most important oil-producing region. Between 1975 and 1995 production dropped nearly 50 per cent from 17 mt/y to 9 mt/y. Oil production declined every year from 1990 to 1997, though 1998 marked the beginning of recovery, with the first new AIOC wells coming into production.[23]

While estimates vary widely and much exploratory work remains to be done, Azerbaijan's recoverable oil reserves may be between 0.5 and 1.5 billion tonnes of oil – compare Nigeria's 2.8 billion tonnes, Russia's 6.8 billion tonnes and Kuwait's 13 billion tonnes.[24] If this proves to be the case, Azerbaijan may be considered to be potentially a medium-sized oil- producing country. Commercially, however, Azerbaijan's attractiveness has lain less in the total reserves than in the Caspian basin's status as the last major unclaimed petroleum territory, and in the fact that successive Baku governments have deliberately set out rapidly to attract international investment by offering favourable contractual terms. These factors, their complex interface with strategic interests (see Chapter 4), and the special export issues involved in Caspian oil production have combined to make Caspian and particularly Azerbaijani petroleum the subject of high-profile and often hectic international interest and manoeuvring in the 1990s.

Since the late Soviet period the potential of the oil industry, given the necessary investment and technology, to generate economic growth in Azerbaijan and, in more optimistic visions, in the whole Caucasus region has been widely recognized.[25] Baku has also calculated that its best chance of engaging foreign interests to counter Russian domination and support Azerbaijani independence and stability is by bringing major foreign investments into the petroleum industry (see Chapter 4). Negotiations with Western oil companies began in 1990, but the Soviet collapse and the political turmoil of the early years of independence meant that deals were long delayed (Suret Huseinov's coup against Elchibey's APF government took place just in time to prevent the signing of a major contract, a fact which many commentators have suspected was more than coincidental, though a causal connection has never been demonstrated).

The first and largest contract was signed in September 1994 between SOCAR (the Azerbaijani state oil company, which is both a party to and responsible for negotiating all contracts) and the AIOC. The consortium's international profile has been subject to slight subsequent changes and now includes US, British, Norwegian, Russian, Turkish, Japanese and Saudi Arabian companies. The agreement covers the Azeri, Chirag and deep-water Guneshli fields, whose estimated reserves are put at half a billion tonnes of oil and 155 bcm of gas. Estimated total investment will be US\$8–10 billion.[26]

Figure 7: Azerbaijan – oil and gas production and forecasts

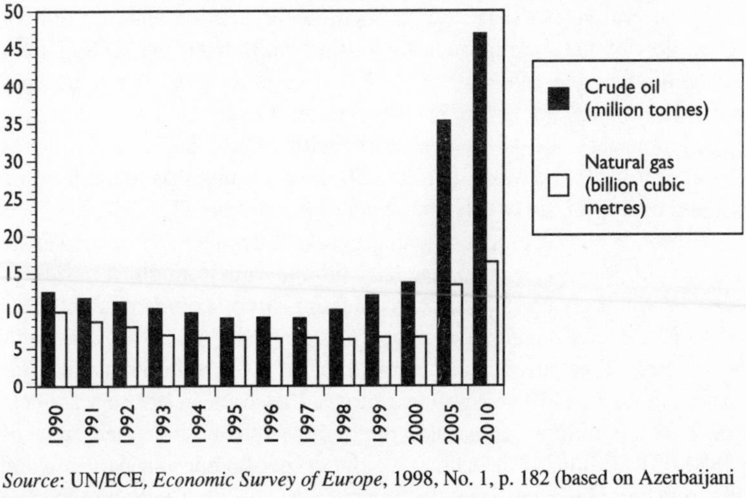

Source: UN/ECE, *Economic Survey of Europe*, 1998, No. 1, p. 182 (based on Azerbaijani government sources).

Figure 8: Foreign direct investment

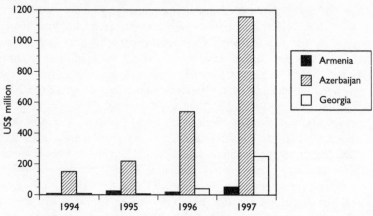

Sources: Armenia Economic Trends; Azerbaijan Economic Trends; Georgia 1994–6: EBRD, *Transition Report Update 1997;* 1997: *Georgian Economic Trends.*

The AIOC agreement marked a watershed in several ways: it brought international companies into Caspian Sea oil development for the first time (thereby igniting the Caspian legal regime dispute); it was the first major foreign investment in Azerbaijan (or the Caucasus); it focused Western interests and policy much more sharply on the Caspian and Azerbaijan; it was not only the first major contract to be signed, but will be by several years the first to start serious production and to require a resolution of the pipeline question. 'Early oil' from the Chirag field began production in November 1997 at a rate of around 1,000 tonnes per day. The 'main oil' from the deep-water Guneshli field will begin production early in the next century, with Azerbaijan's total oil production projected to peak at around 50 million tonnes per annum in the second decade of the twenty-first century (see Figure 7).

A further eleven production-sharing agreements had been signed by summer 1998, involving companies from the same foreign countries, as well as from Italy and France, consolidating strong commercial interests in Azerbaijan for a number of major Western states.

Foreign direct investment in Azerbaijan's oil industry already far exceeds any other investment flows into the Caucasus. In 1997 it accounted for US$780 million of a total direct investment into Azerbaijan of US$1,051 million. In the same year direct investment into Armenia and Georgia combined amounted to a mere $300 million (see Figure 8). The

Figure 9: Azerbaijan – oil-related share of capital and financial account

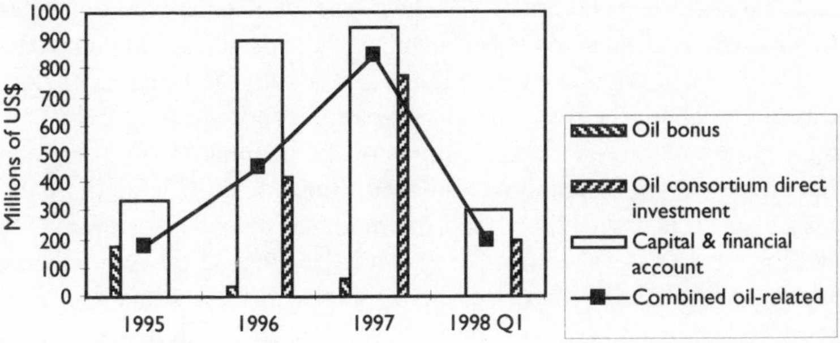

Source: *Azerbaijan Economic Trends.*

oil investment and bonuses dominate in Azerbaijan's capital and financial account, having provided 89 per cent of the total in 1997.

Azerbaijan's medium-term economic prospects appear bright. Future oil income will give the government the potential to balance the budget, maintain a trade surplus, and make substantial investments in infrastructure, non-oil sectors of the economy, appropriate military forces, health, education and cultural provision (see Figure 9). If oil revenue is used prudently, Azerbaijan may emerge in two decades as a securely independent, prosperous state, with a broad-based economy offering good opportunities for its citizens to participate and fulfil their potential. Moreover, a dynamic commercial oil and oil-related services sector will help to transform the entire business environment.

The achievement of such an optimal exploitation of oil resources is, however, far from assured, and the experiences of other oil-rich states offer more negative than positive historical precedents. Among the inherent problems of an oil-based economy are vulnerability to fluctuations in world oil prices, the 'Dutch disease' (the negative effect of a booming oil sector, which tends to raise wage levels, attract workers from other sectors and bolster the currency, all of which damage the competitiveness of other sectors), and problems in managing the fall-off after production has peaked (Baku's precipitate signing of numerous production-sharing agreements is likely to exaggerate the 'bulge' of the production peak). The concentration of revenue at the centre which is characteristic of oil economies requires particular attention to redistribution and to transparency and accountability in government and the oil sector. The apparent tendency towards arbitrariness and authoritarianism in states with an oil-based political economy has been explained as a consequence of the fact that such states do not need to negotiate with society through taxation to secure revenue, to the detriment of healthy state–society relations.

Exaggerated popular expectations of oil wealth can be destabilizing, especially where the distribution of wealth is very uneven, and where the aspirations of significant sections of the population (refugees and IDPs, for example) remain unfulfilled. Sudden oil-generated wealth may also upset the regional and international balance of power. The fear or envy of neighbouring states may be aroused by Azerbaijan's imminent oil-based prosperity; the dispute with Russia and Iran over the Caspian Sea's legal regime may be seen in this light, as may its dispute with Turkmenistan over ownership of certain Caspian Sea oilfields. In the context of the unresolved Karabagh dispute and the absence of normal relations with Armenia, Azerbaijan's sudden influx of oil wealth could have destabilizing and unpredictable consequences, particularly if a large part of it is channelled into military purchases (see Chapter 2).

Pipelines and transport

A natural and historical bridge for trade routes running east–west and north–south, the Caucasus region has in the twentieth century experienced an extraordinary isolation that has denied both geographical configuration and historical tradition.[27] In the Soviet period the region was isolated by the deliberate state policy of strict border controls and the development of infrastructure to link the region with the Union rather than with external states, while in the post-Soviet period wars and the blockades that have persisted long after the signing of ceasefires have maintained the isolation.

Currently the region's main north–south routes (both road and rail), which pass from Iran through Nakhichevan, are obstructed by Azerbaijan's blockade of Armenia, and by the closure of the road and rail routes from Georgia to Russia via Abkhazia. Transit across the Azerbaijani–Russian border was also subject to interruption between 1994 and 1998. The Georgian military highway, which passes through Ossetia to Russia, is open, as are routes from Iran via Azerbaijan to Georgia; and new direct road links between Armenia and Iran have opened up. However, these do not adequately compensate for the loss of the other transit routes, particularly as all the principal north–south rail routes are blocked.

For east–west routes a similar situation prevails: the traditional arteries running east–west along the valley of the River Aras have disappeared ever since it became the Russian–Iranian border in the early nineteenth century. East–west rail links and the most direct and prospective road links between Turkey and the Caucasus are also closed as a result of Ankara's participation in the blockade of Armenia.

The inadequacy of existing infrastructure, especially in circumstances where many of the limited existing links are closed for political reasons, has prompted a number of proposals for reviving the Old Silk Road, building new east–west corridors, reintegrating the transport infrastructure of the CIS republics, or developing new transport networks based on new regional organizations, such as the expanded ECO, BSEC and GUAM. Such proposals are invariably phrased in the language of mutually beneficial regional and international cooperation, but many are clearly designed also to serve the particular political and economic interests of a primary sponsor, with Russia, Turkey and Iran all seeking to reorient the region's transport and communications infrastructure to their own advantage. The politicization of transport issues has been most marked in the pipeline debate (see below). Few of the grandiose transport schemes have any chance of early realization, however, since they are not backed by any investment capital. An important exception is the EU-sponsored TRACECA (Transport Corridor Europe–Caucasus–Asia) scheme, launched in 1993 to develop transport links from western Europe to China via the Caucasus, the Caspian and Central Asia. The EU, the EBRD and the World Bank have all invested significant sums in TRACECA-related projects in Georgia's ports, roads and railways.[28]

Land-locked Armenia, the target of the Azerbaijani–Turkish blockade and the smallest of the Caucasian states, has been hardest hit by the interruption of transport and communications. Its prospects for economic recovery lie in producing for regional export markets and in resuming its historical role as a transit route for north–south and east–west trade. These are both precluded in present circumstances. Armenia also finds itself peripheral to the main thrust of new proposals for east–west corridors linking the Black and Caspian Seas, and to ECO proposals for the development of regional transport links. Yerevan has consistently rejected the idea of trading concessions over Karabagh for a place in Azerbaijan's oil export pipeline system. Kirk Kirkorian is planning to invest US$85 million in highway construction to link Armenia with Georgia's Black Sea ports, and a further US$50 million in road links between Yerevan and Tbilisi, but while these will provide an important boost, in themselves they will not do more than alleviate the isolation caused by the blockade. Diaspora Armenian donations have also paid for the construction of a new road connecting Armenia with Karabagh via the Lachin corridor.

Georgia, by contrast, is the principal beneficiary of plans to develop an east–west corridor, since, with routes through Armenia blockaded, its Black Sea ports and its roads and planned new rail link to Turkey are the only western termini of the Caucasian stretch of the corridor. As a neutral in the Armenian–Azerbaijani conflict, Georgia has also been able to profit as the principal transport partner of both, as well as the main route for the indirect trade of Azerbaijan and Turkey with Armenia. Georgia's important traditional northward routes, however, are themselves subject to blockade.

Azerbaijan also stands to benefit from the development of east–west trade routes, both as a means of freeing its own imports and exports from Russian control, and because of Azerbaijan's own potential role as a transport hub for the Caspian region. Azerbaijan has been lobbying for a permanent TRACECA secretariat to be established in Baku – a presumption of leadership which has ruffled an otherwise cordial understanding with Georgia on the common interests and mutual benefits of developing transport relations. Azerbaijan also suffers from blockades, some of its own making – it has lost the most direct route to Nakhichevan because of the embargo on Armenia, and now has to rely on routes via Iran – and others externally imposed, notably Russian closure or obstruction of their common border from 1994 onwards.

The debate over the routing of pipelines for the export of Azerbaijan's (and potentially other Caspian countries') oil and gas exports has seen the most open expression of the political games underlying the cooperative rhetoric of transport schemes.[29] Armenia, Azerbaijan, Georgia, Russia, Turkey, Iran and the United States have all expressed clear preferences for particular routes for export pipelines. European countries, which are expected to be the main market for Azerbaijan's oil exports, and the AIOC, which will have to find investment for the pipelines, have been much less outspoken. There are undisguised differences of opinion among AIOC consortium member companies. US corporations are more inclined to accommodate Washington's insistence that Iran should be excluded from any significant role in Caspian oil development and that the main pipeline should follow a route via Georgia and Turkey to the Mediterranean. Other companies, led by BP, have been reluctant to allow political concerns to dictate commercial decisions, and have at various times expressed an interest in swap arrangements with Iran and in channelling most or all exports via the cheaper Russian and Georgian routes to the Black Sea.

The decision on the routing of pipelines for Azerbaijan's oil exports is in two stages. The first, on the route for the export of early oil, was reached in autumn 1995, when a compromise solution split early oil exports between Russian and Georgian routes to the Black Sea. While this decision had the benefit of giving something to most of the interested parties (except Iran and Armenia), it merely deferred the final choice of a main route and was criticized by some as excessively expensive and providing unnecessary extra capacity. The decision, due in summer 1997, on the route for a main export line has been continually deferred, partly because of delays in bringing oil-fields into production – there is no urgent commercial need for a decision – and partly because consortium members would prefer to wait until the Georgia–Black Sea pipeline is operational and they can assess the viability of that route. Turkish and US governments have argued hard in favour of the route via Georgia and Turkey, and President Aliyev has also expressed support, but in conditions of low oil prices, commercial arguments for the Russian route, for a re-examination of export via Iran, or for further deferring the decision also appear stronger.

Trade

In spite of the transport blockades and bottlenecks, Armenia, Azerbaijan and Georgia all show a growing propensity to trade.[30] The principal trends in trade are the shift away from former Soviet partners towards regional partners and remote Western partners, and a reshaping of the commodity composition of imports and exports in response to market forces. Armenia, whose trade dependency on Soviet partners was most pronounced, may be used as an example of a pattern that is broadly shared by Azerbaijan and Georgia (see Figures 10 and 11). In 1988, 98 per cent of Armenia's exports went to other Soviet republics and 82 per cent of imports came from them. In 1997, only 41 per cent of exports went to CIS states and only 34 per cent of imports came from them.

A more detailed analysis of recent trade figures (which are perhaps the most defective of all the major recorded statistical data) suggests that this pattern may be bottoming out. Between 1992 and 1997 Azerbaijan's export and import patterns reveal a slight overall shift away from CIS partners (other than Georgia), but nothing resembling the dramatic reorientation of earlier years. The countries of the European Union, Turkey and Iran

Figure 10: Armenia – direction of exports

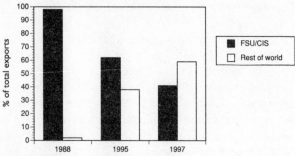

Source: UN/ECE, *Economic Survey of Europe.*

Figure 11: Armenia – direction of imports

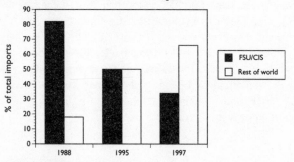

Source: UN/ECE, *Economic Survey of Europe.*

have all intensified their trade relations with the Caucasian countries (see Figures 12 and 13).

All three countries run trade deficits (see Figure 14). Armenia's widened rapidly until the end of 1997. It reached US$623 million over the twelve months to June of that year, equivalent to nearly 40 per cent of GDP, a very high rate even compared to other CIS states. Armenia's external debt reached US$700 million in early 1998. Two-thirds of foreign debt is owed to IFIs (the IMF, the World Bank and the EBRD), while Russia accounts for 15 per cent, the United States and EU combined for nearly as much and Turkmenistan for 4 per cent. Georgia's trade deficit appears more stable at around US$350 million, but it too has a serious foreign debt problem, accumulating some US$1 billion in the period 1991–4, largely for gas imports. Debt servicing and negotiating rescheduling have presented serious difficulties. Azerbaijan's trade deficit is high, 22 per cent of GDP in 1996, falling to 15 per cent in 1997,

Figure 12: Azerbaijan – export distribution by selected countries

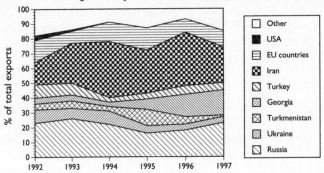

Source: *Azerbaijan Economic Trends*.

Figure 13: Azerbaijan – import distribution by selected countries

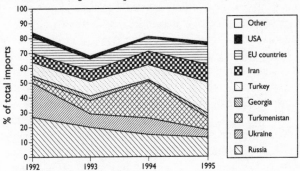

Source: *Azerbaijan Economic Trends*.

Figure 14: Trade balances

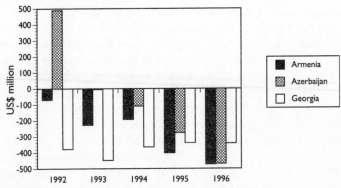

Source: EBRD, *Transition Report*.

but the certainty of future oil revenues means that this causes relatively little concern either in Baku or among the IFS. The biggest creditor is Turkey, followed by Russia and the IFIs. All three states hope to join the World Trade Organization, Armenia having applied in 1993, Georgia in 1996 and Azerbaijan in 1997.

Economy and society

Human capital is one of the principal resources of all three Caucasian states. The Soviet welfare system and industrial experience produced a generally healthy workforce (except for the populations of areas suffering acute environmental degradation, such as Sumgait in Azerbaijan), that was educated and skilled, with both men and women participating fully in the labour market.

Sustaining the level of human capital presents a major challenge for all three states.[31] Wars and conflicts have caused large-scale displacement of population (see Chapter 2), with refugees and IDPs often living in very harsh conditions and without adequate educational or healthcare facilities. In Azerbaijan and Georgia there are signs of the emergence of an IDP underclass. In addition a great many people have migrated out of the region for economic motives. Quantifying this trend is very difficult, since no censuses have been taken since the last Soviet census of 1989. Unofficial estimates place the number of emigrants from Georgia at between 800,000 and one million (some 20 per cent of the population), and from Armenia at around 5–800,000 (between a sixth and a quarter of the population). Remittances from emigrants make an important economic contribution, but migration takes some of the best-qualified people out of the domestic labour market and produces a gender imbalance. Russia's 1998 crisis has had a serious impact on both Armenia and Georgia, reducing the incomes of families dependent on remittances, and weakening the budget and currency situation.

Education and healthcare provision has deteriorated markedly since independence, with government more or less abdicating its role to allow an informal privatization.[32] Benefits of all kinds are very low and often in arrears. The low level of unemployment benefit as well as other disincentives to registration account for the small number of registered unemployed. The figures certainly understate the problem, which is partly obscured by the retention of workers on the payroll at inactive enterprises. Though real wages are rising in all three countries, rates remain low – only Armenia has set an indexed minimum wage – and for both state- and private-sector employees are often paid in arrears.

Income distribution has become more unequal and poverty has increased. In Georgia in 1997 the richest fifth of the population earned eleven times more than the poorest, while only the top two-fifths had consumption above the minimum subsistence level. The UN Human Development Index places Armenia 103rd, Georgia 105th and Azerbaijan 106th out of 121 countries.[33] For much of the 1990s provision for the poorer sections of society has been possible only through large-scale inflows of humanitarian assistance.

Regional variations in living conditions are becoming more pronounced, as market economics allow investment and growth to concentrate in areas enjoying comparative advantage. In all respects living and economic conditions in the secessionist republics of Karabagh and Abkhazia are more depressed than elsewhere in the region.[34]

Summing up

Armenia, Azerbaijan and Georgia have all successfully stabilized after catastrophic economic collapse. The macroeconomic policies adopted by all three governments show a high degree of similarity – partly because of the normative influence of IFI advisers and Western technical assistance – and also a high degree of success in achieving their objectives. Those policies do not, in themselves, however, assure sustainable growth, while they have entailed heavy living standards costs for most citizens. The similarities in the situations and policies of the three states have been close enough to produce patterns of development which are shared by the Caucasian states, and which mark them off from other post-Soviet and transition economies. Armenia and Georgia have been generally a year or two ahead of Azerbaijan in their reforms.

The challenge now facing each of the countries is to transform macroeconomic stability and the initial turn-around from recession into sustained growth that can start to recover the enormous economic losses inflicted in the early 1990s. None of the three states have yet progressed very far along this road. In Armenia, which led the way with its macroeconomic and structural reforms, growth has faltered in conditions of continuing blockade, especially when the commitment to economic reform was not strong enough to dislodge powerful vested interests. The new government portrays itself as committed to liberalizing economic reform and its first year (1998) saw some developments in large-scale privatization and foreign investment (partly from diaspora sources), but the commitment seems only skin-deep, with vested interests still blocking reform. It seems inevitable that Armenia's economic potential will be frustrated until the Karabagh conflict is resolved and the blockade by Azerbaijan and Turkey lifted.

While Azerbaijan's structural reforms remain less developed, it has an outstanding economic resource in its oil reserves, and these are drawing major foreign investment, even if the business environment is in many ways forbidding. Accelerating oil-based economic development seems virtually assured, though the regime's capacity to manage that development effectively to secure long-term economic, social and political stability is far from certain.

Georgia also has an important advantage as a terminus on the new transport routes stretching east–west from China to Europe. In terms of structural reform and business environment it now appears the most developed of the Caucasian states, though major weaknesses in taxation and foreign debt remain.

The comparative advantages enjoyed by Azerbaijan and Georgia, coupled with Armenia's economic isolation, seem likely to produce an increasingly differentiated pattern of development, with Azerbaijan surging ahead and Armenia lagging behind. Such a scenario assumes, however, that domestic and international political variables remain constant, and that is a very uncertain assumption. All three Caucasian states remain vulnerable to resumption of conflict or political instability, but in this respect Armenia tends to enjoy a comparative advantage, having achieved a relatively high degree of stability, sustained during the transition from one president to the next.

For Armenia and Georgia, and for the non-oil sector in Azerbaijan, the opening up of regional markets is vital, since national markets are so small. Denser trade relations and deepening regional cooperation, or even integration, would benefit all three states but until political constraints are removed these changes are unlikely to occur.

Chapter 6

Conclusion

The last decade has been a period of radical and often violent change in the Caucasus, and for much of it governments, communities, enterprises and individuals have been obliged to concentrate on immediate survival. At the same time the break-up of the Soviet Union and the restoration of Caucasian independence have urgently demanded attention to major long-term issues: the relationship between statehood, nationhood, territory and citizenship; the constitutional models and institutional mechanisms for regulating relations between state and society, between centre and periphery, and between titular and minority communities; the location of the Caucasus in the international system; and the balance of national, market and social priorities in economic development.

The challenges faced by Armenia, Azerbaijan and Georgia have been similar to those confronting other post-communist states, but in the Caucasus the challenges have presented themselves with peculiar intensity, owing to the region's specific historical and cultural characteristics and its strategic significance. The immensity of the challenges and the paucity of available resources have at times threatened to precipitate state failure. Georgia came closest to complete collapse in the anarchy and civil war of 1993, but Armenia approached the economic brink in the winter of 1992–3, while the viability of the Azerbaijani state also was called into question by military defeat and internal power struggles in 1993–4. Against this background, and in the light of the doom-laden prognoses of many analysts in the early 1990s, the mere survival of the three south Caucasian states may be considered an achievement.

In fact, much more has been achieved. By any measure the current situation of Armenia, Azerbaijan and Georgia is a great improvement on that of 1993. Far from a downward spiral into escalating internecine conflict, lasting cease-fires have been established in the Karabagh, South Ossetian and Abkhazian conflicts. Constitutions and the fundamental political institutions of independent states have been established. Economies have stabilized and are beginning to recover from disastrous decline. The international balance of power has become more favourable for Caucasian independence, and international engagement is supporting reform processes and encouraging the spread of normative standards into the region.

Certainly progress remains uneven, and failures are not hard to identify. Authoritarianism, corruption, stalled peace negotiations, widening wealth distribution, and collapsing social provision are as characteristic of the 'new' Caucasus as the positive attributes just mentioned. Whether the current situation is pronounced to be achievement or failure depends ultimately as much on the expectations of the judge as on the performance of the region. Whatever the verdict, the existing status quo remains fragile and unsustainable in the medium term. Today's political stability depends on the persons of ageing presidents; cease-fires are a product of transient configurations of military balance and international support; further structural reform is needed before economic development can become self-sustaining; and international forces may realign in a balance less favourable for the region. A continuation of the rapid pace of change of recent years is, therefore, not only to be predicted but to be welcomed.

Key political priorities for the coming years are the development of state–society relations, of civil society and of a civic, rather than ethnic, concept of citizenship. The elaboration of an institutional framework for relations between titular and minority communities must be a part of any lasting settlement of the region's conflicts. Fuller exploitation of citizens' economic potential and more effective redistributive mechanisms to support human resources are vital for any sustainable economic recovery. Internationally, the cultivation of diverse mutually beneficial relations and the engagement of multiple international interests in the region require a regional counterpart of cooperation among all three Caucasian states. Initiatives to re-establish the region's role as a bridge for Eurasian transport and communications must also recognize the need for inclusive, positive-sum projects for north–south as well as east–west connections.

Progress towards achieving these will depend in part on developments in Armenia, Azerbaijan and Georgia. This requires effective leadership, capable of identifying long-term objectives and mobilizing political and other resources to attain them, but that is only likely to emerge in a context of wider public and political debate. Other factors which may have a decisive bearing on the region's development are outside the control of the Caucasian states. Political and economic developments in Russia and consequent shifts in Russian foreign policy are a volatile but crucial element in regional dynamics. To a lesser degree internal developments in Turkey and Iran and their foreign policy implications are important. Western policy also is significant since it underpins the IFI engagement in the Caucasus. US decisions about the priority given to different foreign policy areas can also make a strong impact.

The extraction and export of Azerbaijan's oil is another factor which will profoundly affect the region's development. How Azerbaijan manages this resource and the revenues it generates will shape the trajectory of domestic economic and political development, as well as the potential for regional cooperation. How external players manage their commercial competition and strategic interests in Caspian oil will decide whether the international dynamic will be a positive-sum or a zero-sum game.

Regional conflict, however, remains the single most important factor in deciding whether the Caucasus countries' independence and economic development will prove sustainable. Conflict resolution presents the greatest test for the Caucasian states, since the conflicts are entangled in all aspects of their development. In the political arena, an inclusive vision of the nation, accountable and law-abiding government, and respect for human rights are essential for a peaceful resolution to the conflicts, while, conversely, failure to reach a settlement constrains political development in these directions. In international terms, an environment in which external actors see their interests as lying in Caucasian peace and stability is a prerequisite for settlement, while continuing conflict will provide opportunities for interference and manipulation by external actors playing zero-sum games for control over the region. Economic development and prosperity can provide incentives for the parties to resolve their differences and can underpin any settlement with economic rewards; but without resolution of the conflicts, key resources will continue to lie unexploited, the region's political risk will remain high, and trade relations and regional economic cooperation will continue to be distorted and depressed by blockades.

Notes

Chapter 2: Politics

1 There is an extensive academic literature on Soviet and post-Soviet nationality and nationalism. See G. Smith et al., *Nation-building in the Post-Soviet Borderlands: The Politics of National Identities* (Cambridge: CUP, 1998); G. Smith (ed.), *The Nationalities Question in the Post-Soviet States* (London: Longman, 2nd edition 1996); I. Bremmer and R. Taras (eds), *New States, New Politics: Building the Post-Soviet Nations* (Cambridge: CUP, 2nd edition, 1997); V. Tishkov, *Ethnicity, Nationalism and Conflict in and after the Soviet Union: The Mind Aflame* (London: Sage, 1997); R.G. Suny, *The Revenge of the Past: Nationalism, Revolution, and the Collapse of the Soviet Union* (Stanford, CA: Stanford University Press, 1993); M. Saroyan, 'Beyond the Nation-State: Culture and Ethnic Politics in Soviet Transcaucasia', in R.G. Suny (ed.), *Transcaucasia, Nationalism, and Social Change: Essays in the History of Armenia, Azerbaijan and Georgia* (Ann Arbor: University of Michigan Press, revised edition 1996), pp. 401–26.

2 B. A. Anderson and B. D. Silver, 'Population Redistribution and the Ethnic Balance in Transcaucasia', in R.G. Suny (ed.), *Transcaucasia, Nationalism, and Social Change*, p. 495.

3 P. Rutland, 'Democracy and Nationalism in Armenia', *Europe–Asia Studies* (46/5,1995), p. 842.

4 M. Saroyan, 'The Karabagh Syndrome and Azerbaijani Politics', *Problems of Communism* (39/1, 1990), pp. 14–29.

5 S. Jones and R. Parsons, 'Georgia and the Georgians', in G. Smith (ed.), *The Nationalities Question in the Post-Soviet States*, pp. 298–9.

6 N. Dudwick, 'Political Transformations in Postcommunist Armenia: Images and Realities', in K. Dawisha and B. Parrot (eds), *Conflict, Cleavage, and Change in Central Asia and the Caucasus* (Cambridge: CUP, 1997), pp. 79–80.

7 Rutland, 'Democracy and Nationalism', pp. 851–4.

8 J. Aves, 'Politics, Parties and Presidents in Transcaucasia', *Caucasian Regional Studies* (1, 1996), p. 5.

9 J. Aves, *Georgia: From Chaos to Stability?* (London: RIIA, Former Soviet South Paper, 1996), pp. 38–49; E. Fuller, 'Azerbaijan at the Crossroads', in R. Allison (ed.), *Challenges for the Former Soviet South* (Washington and London: Brookings/RIIA, 1996), pp. 144–5.

10 E. Fuller, 'Paramilitary Forces Dominate Fighting in Transcaucasus', *RFE/ RL Research Report* (2/25, 1993), pp. 74–82.

11 Aves, 'Politics, Parties and Presidents', p. 9.

12 E. Fuller, 'Azerbaijan's June Revolution', *RFE/RL Research Report* (2/32, 1993).

13 Fuller, 'Azerbaijan at the Crossroads', p. 128; J. Aves, 'Post-Soviet Transcaucasia', in R. Allison (ed.), *Challenges for the Former Soviet South*, pp. 205–7.

14 OMRI, *Daily Digest* (12/ Part I, 17 January 1997).

15 Aves, 'Post-Soviet Transcaucasia', p. 209.

16 D. Slider, 'Georgia', in G.E. Curtis (ed.), *Armenia, Azerbaijan, and Georgia: Country Studies* (Washington: Library of Congress, 1995), pp. 169–70; Aves, 'Politics, Parties and Presidents', pp. 13–14.

17 Aves, 'Politics, Parties and Presidents', pp. 15–17.

18 These are the nicknames in most common use in Armenia, Azerbaijan and Georgia.

19 Dudwick, 'Political Transformations in Postcommunist Armenia', pp. 89–91; I. Bremmer and C. Welt, 'Armenia's New Autocrats', *Journal of Democracy* (8/3, 1997), pp. 81–5.

20 Bremmer and Welt, 'Armenia's New Autocrats', p. 84.

21 The current constitutions of all three countries were adopted in 1995. English texts are given in: The International Institute for Democracy (ed.), *Transition to Democracy: Constitutions of the New Independent States and Mongolia* (Strasbourg: Council of Europe, 1997).

22 Parliamentary elections were held in Armenia and Azerbaijan in 1995, and in Georgia in 1992 and 1995. Presidential elections were held in Azerbaijan in 1992, 1993 and 1998, in Georgia in 1991 and 1995, and in Armenia in 1991, 1996 and 1998.

23 Aves, *Georgia: From Chaos to Stability?*, pp. 6–10, 13–14; Slider,

'Georgia', pp. 213–18. For recent internal criticisms of the constitution see RFE/RL, *Caucasus Report* (1/23, 4 August 1998).

24 Bremmer and Welt, 'Armenia's New Autocrats', p. 87.

25 USA, Commission on Security and Cooperation in Europe, *Report on Azerbaijan's November 1995 Parliamentary Election* (Washington, 1996).

26 *Svobodnaya Gruziya*, 19 October 1995, cited in Aves, *Georgia: From Chaos to Stability?*, p. 7.

27 Jamestown Foundation, *Monitor* (4/123, 26 June 1998).

28 S. Jones, 'Populism in Georgia: the Gamsaxurdia Phenomenon', in D.V. Schartz and R. Panossian, *Nationalism and History: The Politics of Nation Building in Post-Soviet Armenia, Azerbaijan and Georgia* (Toronto: University of Toronto Press, 1994), pp. 130–37; D. Zurabishvili, 'Shevardnadze's One-man Democracy', *War Report* (45, 1996), pp. 30–32.

29 On Ter-Petrosian, Aliyev and Shevardnadze, see E. Fuller in *Building Democracy: The OMRI Annual Survey of Eastern Europe and the Former Soviet Union 1995* (New York: M.E. Sharpe, 1996), pp. 252–3, 258–9, 264–5.

30 RFE/RL, *Caucasus Report* (1/27, 2 September 1998).

31 In recent years the international organization playing the leading role in organizing observer missions for Caucasian elections has been the OSCE's Office of Democratic Institutions and Human Rights. OSCE final election reports, in contrast to some others, are based on the findings of coordinated nationwide observation.

32 RFE/RL, *Caucasus Report* (1/33, 16 October 1998).

33 The European Institute for the Media produces regular reports on media coverage of elections.

34 Dudwick, 'Political Transformations in Postcommunist Armenia', pp. 84–9.

35 Detailed accounts of human rights issues in Armenia, Azerbaijan and Georgia can be found in the publications of Amnesty International, Human Rights Watch/Helsinki Watch, Freedom House and the US Department of State's *Annual Country Reports* on human rights practices.

36 Dudwick, 'Political Transformations in Postcommunist Armenia', p. 98.

37 Ibid., pp. 74–5; D. Zurabishvili, 'Shevardnadze's One-man Democracy', pp. 30–31.

38 R.G. Suny, 'Elite Transformation in Late-Soviet and Post-Soviet Transcaucasia, or What Happens When the Ruling Class Can't Rule?', in T.J. Colton and R.C. Tucker (eds), *Patterns in Post-Soviet Leadership* (Boulder, CO, San Francisco and Oxford: Westview Press, 1995), p. 141.

Chapter 3: Conflicts and security

1 J. Aves, *Georgia: From Chaos to Stability?* (London: RIIA, 1996), pp. 46–9;
   I. Rotar, 'Mingrelia: Georgia's New "Hot Spot"', Jamestown Foundation,
   Prism (4/8, 17 April 1998).
2 J. Aves, *Georgia: From Chaos to Stability?*, pp. 41–4; Z. Anjaparidze,
   'Storm Clouds in Ajaria?', Jamestown Foundation, *Prism* (3/19, 21
   November 1997); RFE/RL, *Caucasus Report* (1/31, 30 September 1998).
3 J. Aves, *Georgia: From Chaos to Stability?*, pp. 44–6; D. Darchiashvili,
   'The Army and Society in Djavakheti', *The Army and Society in Georgia*
   (May 1998); I. Rotar, 'Tbilisi Has Only Partial Control over Georgia's
   Armenian Regions', Jamestown Foundation, *Prism* (4/10, 15 May 1998).
4 A. Matveeva, *Dagestan*, FSS Briefing No. 13 (London: RIIA, 1997);
   E. Fuller, 'The Lezgin Hostage-taking: Background on Sadval', *OMRI
   Analytical Brief* (266, 15 July 1996); *Inside Central Asia* (2–8 June 1997),
   p. 6.
5 See P. Baev, *Russia's Policies in the Caucasus* (London: RIIA, 1997),
   Chapter 5, 'Russia's Military Policies in the Caucasus'; D. Trenin,
   'Russia's Security Interests and Policies in the Caucasus Region', in
   B. Coppieters (ed.), *Contested Borders in the Caucasus* (Brussels: VUB
   Press, 1996), pp. 91–102.
6 M. Webber, *CIS Integration Trends: Russia and the Former Soviet South*
   (London: RIIA, 1997), pp. 34–47; Baev, *Russia's Policies in the Caucasus*,
   pp. 23–29; W.E. Odom and R. Dujarric, *Commonwealth or Empire?
   Russia, Central Asia and the Transcaucasus* (Indianapolis, IN: Hudson
   Institute, 1995), pp. 29–34.
7 See R. Allison and Christoph Bluth (eds), *Security Dilemmas in Russia and
   Eurasia* (London: RIIA, 1998).
8 V.V. Naumkin and I.D. Zviagelskaya, 'The Southern Tier: Non-Traditional
   Threats, Challenges and Risks for Russia's Security', in R. Menon, Yu.
   Federov and G. Nodia, *Russia, the Caucasus and Central Asia: The 21st
   Century Security Environment* (Armonk, NY: M.E. Sharpe, forthcoming
   1999).
9 For a discussion of these issues in the context of Russian policy towards
   Central Asia, see L. Jonson, *Russia and Central Asia: A New Web of
   Relations* (London: RIIA, 1998).
10 Institute for Strategic Studies, *The Military Balance 1998/99* (Oxford: IISS/
   OUP, 1998), p. 85.
11 S.N. MacFarlane et al., *Armed Conflict in Georgia: A Case Study in
   Humanitarian Action and Peacekeeping* (Providence, RI: Thomas J. Watson
   Jr. Institute for International Studies, Occasional Paper No. 21, 1996).

12 J.R. Masih and R.O. Krikorian, *Armenia at the Crossroads* (Amsterdam: Harwood Academic Publishers, forthcoming 1999), pp. 99–101.

13 J. Aves, 'The Caucasus States: The Regional Security Complex', in Allison and Bluth (eds), *Security Dilemmas in Russia and Eurasia*, pp. 175–87.

14 The approach survived Gamsakhurdia's ouster and Shevardnadze's return, continuing until autumn 1993.

15 For accounts of the development of the Armenian, Azerbaijani and Georgian armies see: Odom and Dujarric, *Commonwealth or Empire?*, pp. 77–8, 82–3, 87–8; A. Zverev, 'Ethnic Conflicts in the Caucasus 1988–94', in Coppieters (ed.), *Contested Borders in the Caucasus*, p. 35; J. Aves, 'The Caucasus States'.

16 *The Military Balance 1998/99*, p. 74.

17 M. Gaume, 'After the War', *Armenian International Magazine* (August 1998), pp. 30–31.

18 *The Military Balance 1998/99*, pp. 75–6.

19 *The Military Balance 1998/99*, p. 85.

20 *The Military Balance 1998/99*, p. 76.

21 *The Military Balance 1998/99*, p. 85.

22 B. Coppieters, 'Conclusions: The Caucasus as a Security Complex', in B. Coppieters (ed.), *Contested Borders in the Caucasus*, pp. 193–204.

23 F. Hill, *Report on Ethnic Conflict in the Russian Federation and Transcaucasia* (Cambridge MA: Harvard University, John F. Kennedy School of Government, Strengthening Democratic Institutions Project, 1993), pp. 108–11; Zverev, 'Ethnic Conflicts in the Caucasus', pp. 50–51; T. Kuzio, 'The Chechnya Crisis and the "Near Abroad"', *Central Asian Survey* (14/4,1995), pp. 568–9.

24 R. Allison, 'The Network of New Security Policy Relations in Eurasia' and 'The Chechenia Conflict: Military and Security Policy Implications', in Allison and Bluth (eds), *Security Dilemmas for Russia and Eurasia*, pp. 18–19, 257–67.

25 See 'National Identity and the Myths of Ethnogenesis in Transcaucasia', in G. Smith et al., *Nation-building in the Post-Soviet Borderlands: The Politics of National Identities* (Cambridge: CUP, 1998), pp. 48–66.

26 See the sources cited in Chapter 2, Note 1; also B.G. Hewitt, 'The Role of Scholars in the Abkhazians' Loss of Trust in the Georgians and How to Remedy the Situation', in M. Tütüncü (ed.), *Caucasus: War and Peace* (Haarlem: SOTA, 1998), pp. 115–25; and G.A. Bournoutian, 'Rewriting History: Recent Azeri Alterations of Primary Sources Dealing with Karabakh', *Journal of the Society for Armenian Studies* (6, 1992–3), pp. 185–90.

27 H. Hannum, 'Self-Determination in the Post-Colonial Era', in D. Clark and R. Williamson (eds), *Self-Determination: International Perspectives* (Basingstoke and London: Macmillan, 1996), pp. 22, 25–31.

28 I. Brownlie (ed.), *Basic Documents on Human Rights* (Oxford: OUP, 3rd edition 1992), p. 396.

29 I. Rotar, 'Abkhazia: a New "Criminal Enclave" in the Former Soviet Union?', in Jamestown Foundation, *Prism* (3/10, 27 June 1997).

30 Karabagh is a territory of some 4,400 sq. km. In 1979 its population was 162,000 (76 per cent Armenian; 23 per cent Azeri). Of approximately 350,000 Armenians then living in Azerbaijan, 123,000 lived in Karabagh.

31 N. Dudwick, 'Nagorno-Karabakh and the Politics of Sovereignty', in R.G. Suny (ed.) *Transcaucasia, Nationalism, and Social Change: Essays in the History of Armenia, Azerbaijan and Georgia* (revised edition, Ann Arbor, MI,: University of Michigan Press, 1996), pp. 427–40.

32 *CIS Migration Report* (Geneva: International Organization for Migration, 1997) pp. 11–31; E.W. Walker. *No Peace, No War in the Caucasus: Secessionist Conflict in Chechnya, Abkhazia and Nagorno-Karabagh* (Cambridge, MA: Harvard University, John F. Kennedy School of Government, Strengthening Democratic Institutions Project, 1998), p. 29. On the problems of establishing the facts about the expulsions, see A.F. Fogelquist, 'Assessing the Origins of the Karabakh Conflict', in Tütüncü (ed.), *Caucasus: War and Peace*, pp. 12–16.

33 Walker, *No Peace, No War in the Caucasus*, p. 28.

34 Walker, *No Peace, No War in the Caucasus*, p. 26.

35 South Ossetia has a territory of 3,900 sq. km. In 1989 its population was 99,000 (67 per cent Ossete; 29 per cent Georgian). Of 164,000 Ossetes living in Georgia, 65,000 lived in South Ossetia.

36 Hill, *Report on Ethnic Conflict in the Russian Federation and Transcaucasia*, p. 96.

37 Zverev, 'Ethnic Conflicts in the Caucasus 1988–1994', pp. 45, 47.

38 *CIS Migration Report*, pp. 48–9.

39 D. Sammut, *Confidence Building Matters: the Birth of the Georgian State: Giving Georgia a Second Chance* (London: VERTIC, 1994); MacFarlane et al., *Armed Conflict in Georgia: A Case Study in Humanitarian Action and Peacekeeping* (Providence, RI: Thomas J. Watson Jr Institute for International Studies, Occasional Paper No. 21, 1996).

40 Abkhazia has a territory of 8,600 sq. km. In 1989 its population was 537,000 (46 per cent Georgian; 18 per cent Abkhaz; 15 per cent Armenian; 14 per cent Russian).

41 On the complexity of the language/ethnicity issue in Georgia, see B.G.

Hewitt, 'Abkhazia: a Problem of Identity and Ownership', in J.F.R. Wright et al., *Transcaucasian Boundaries* (London: UCL Press, 1996), p. 191; and R. Gachechiladze, *The New Georgia: Space, Society Politics* (London: UCL Press, 1995), pp. 17, 75–8. In the present study 'Georgian' is used in the imprecise, but generally accepted, wider sense, to include Mingrelian and Svan. The latter peoples are registered as Georgians on their passports, share the Georgian written language (though Mingrelian and Svan both survive as spoken languages) and are mostly content to be identified as Georgians. The overwhelming majority of 'Georgians' in Abkhazia were Mingrelians.

42 G. Nodia, 'The Conflict in Abkhazia: National Projects and Political Circumstances', in B. Coppieters et al. (eds), *Georgians and Abkhazians: The Search for a Peace Settlement* (Cologne: BIOst, 1998), pp. 14–48.

43 V.A. Chirikba, 'Georgian–Abkhazian Conflict and its Aftermath', in Tütüncü (ed.), *Caucasus: War and Peace*, p. 73.

44 G. Otyrba, 'War in Abkhazia: the Regional Significance of the Georgian–Abkhazian Conflict', in R. Szporluk (ed.), *National Identity and Ethnicity in Russia and the New States of Eurasia* (Armonk, NY: M.E. Sharpe, *The Internaional Politics of Eurasia*,Vol. 2, 1994), p. 286.

45 Ibid., pp. 294–7; P. Overeem, 'Report of a UNPO co-ordinated human rights mission to Abkhazia and Georgia', *Central Asian Survey.* (14/1, 1995), pp. 127–54.

46 Russia also equipped the Georgian forces. Local Russian units and their commanders, as well as generals in Moscow, made ad hoc decisions based on personal preferences and local loyalties, with scant regard for official policy. D. Lynch, *The Conflict in Abkhazia: Dilemmas in Russian 'Peacekeeping' Policy* (London: RIIA, Discussion Paper 77, 1998), pp. 26–7; Zverev, 'Ethnic Conflicts in the Caucasus 1988–1994', pp. 49, 51–5; Nodia, 'The Conflict in Abkhazia', pp 38–43.

47 Lynch, *The Conflict in Abkhazia*, p. 30.

48 Walker, *No Peace, No War in the Caucasus*, p. 15.

49 S. Jones, 'The Georgian–Abkhazian Dispute: A Hot Summer', *Analysis of Current Events.* (9/6, 1997), p. 10.

50 Z. Anjaparidze, 'Negotiability Versus Negotiations: Georgia and the Abkhaz Question', Jamestown Foundation, *Prism* (4/6, 20 March 1998).

51 Walker, *No Peace, No War in the Caucasus*, p. 17; Jones, 'The Georgian–Abkhazian Dispute', pp. 10–11.

Chapter 4: International relations

1 R.G. Suny, 'Living with the Other: Conflict and Co-operation among the Transcaucasian Peoples', in S.M. Antounian (ed.), *The Transcaucasus Today: Prospects for Regional Integration*, 23–25 June 1997, Edited Conference Report (Yerevan: American University of Armenia, no date), pp. 52–3.

2 Commercial and official interest in this subject has generated a considerable volume of analysis. Among interesting contributions are J. Roberts, *Caspian Pipelines* (London: RIIA, 1996); R. Forsythe, *The Politics of Oil in the Caucasus and Central Asia: Problems, Prospects and Policy*, Adelphi Paper 300 (London: International Institute for Strategic Studies, 1996); R. Menon, 'Treacherous Terrain: the Political and Security Dimensions of Energy Development in the Caspian Sea Zone', *Analysis* (9/1, National Bureau of Asian Research, Seattle), February 1998; V. Shorokhov, 'Energy Resources of Azerbaijan: Political Stability and Regional Relations', *Caucasian Regional Studies* (1, 1996), pp. 37–70; R. Cutler, 'Towards Co-operative Energy Security in the South Caucasus', *Caucasian Regional Studies* (1, 1996), pp. 71–81; L. Ruseckas, 'State of the Field Report: Energy and Politics in Central Asia and the Caucasus', *Access Asia Review* (1/2, National Bureau of Asian Research, Seattle); *The Geopolitics of Oil, Gas, and Ecology in the Caucasus and Caspian Basin*, Report of a Conference held on 16 May 1998 (Berkeley Program in Soviet and Post-Soviet Studies, University of California, Berkeley).

3 On Armenia's foreign policy see: J.R. Masih and R.O. Krikorian, in 'Armenia's Foreign Policy', in *Armenia at the Crossroads* (Amsterdam: Harwood Academic Publishers, forthcoming 1999), Chapter 4; R.G. Hovannisian, 'Historical Memory and Foreign Relations: the Armenian Perspective', in S.F. Starr (ed.), *The Legacy of History in Russia and the New States of Eurasia* (Armonk, NY: M.E. Sharpe, *The International Politics of Eurasia*, Vol. 1, 1994), pp. 237–76; R.P. Adalian, 'Armenia's Foreign Policy: Defining Priorities and Coping with Conflict', in A. and K. Dawisha (eds), *The Making of Foreign Policy in Russia and the New States of Eurasia* (Armonk, NY: M.E. Sharpe, *The International Politics of Eurasia*, Vol. 4, 1995), pp. 309–39; G. Ter-Gabrielian and A. Nedolian, 'Armenia: Crossroads or Faultline of Civilizations?', *The International Spectator* (32, April–June 1997) pp. 93–116; E. Danielyan, 'Armenia's Foreign Policy: Balancing between East and West', *Prism* (4/2, 23 January 1998).

4 On relations with the diaspora see the cover story in *Armenian International Magazine* (July 1998), pp. 10–17.

5   On Azerbaijan's foreign policy see: T. Swietochowski, 'Azerbaijan's
    Triangular Relationship: The Land Between Russia, Turkey and Iran', in
    A. Banuazizi and M. Weiner (eds), *The New Geopolitics of Central Asia
    and its Borderlands* (London: I.B. Tauris, 1994), pp 118–35; L. Alieva,
    'The Institutions, Orientations, and Conduct of Foreign Policy in Post-
    Soviet Azerbaijan', in A. and K. Dawisha (eds), *The Making of Foreign
    Policy in Russia and the New States of Eurasia*, pp. 286–308; E.M. Herzig,
    'Azerbaijan's Foreign Policy: Implications for Regional Co-operation', in
    S.M. Antounian (ed.), *The Transcaucasus Today: Prospects for Regional
    Integration* (Yerevan: American University of Armenia, no date), pp. 29–
    33.

6   On Georgia's international relations see: Darrell Slyder, 'Georgia', in G.E.
    Curtis (ed.), *Armenia, Azerbaijan and Georgia: Country Studies*
    (Washington: Library of Congress, 1995), pp. 219–25; A.M. Gegeshidze,
    'Georgia's Foreign Policy: Objectives, Results and Prospects', in
    Antounian (ed.), *The Transcaucasus Today*, pp. 22–8.

7   E. Fuller, 'Introducing the Other GUAM', *RFE/RL Newsline* (169,
    1 December 1997).

8   See P. Baev, *Russia's Policies in the Caucasus* (London: RIIA, 1997).

9   For a discussion of the same issues with regard to Russia's Central Asia
    policy, see L. Jonson, *Russia and Central Asia: A New Web of Relations*
    (London: RIIA, 1998).

10 Baev (*Russia's Policies in the Caucasus*, p. 4) prefers 'post-imperialist';
    M. Light, 'Russia and Transcaucasia', in J.F.R. Wright et al. (eds),
    Transcaucasian Boundaries (London: UCL Press, 1996), pp. 41–6; S. De
    Spiegeleire, 'Russian Responses to Possible EU Policy Initiatives in the
    Caucasus' (Conflict Prevention Network Paper, Stiftung Wissenschaft und
    Politik, Ebenhausen), p. 4 and note 8.

11 See Baev, *Russia's Policies in the Caucasus*, pp. 3–7; De Spiegeleire,
    'Russian Responses', pp. 4–6.

12 De Spiegeleire, 'Russian Responses', pp. 6–11.

13 A. Matveeva, *The North Caucasus: Russia's Fragile Borderland* (London:
    RIIA, 1999).

14 Baev, *Russia's Policies in the Caucasus*, p. 3.

15 Ibid.; M. Mesbahi, 'Russia and the Geopolitics of the Muslim South', in
    M. Mesbahi (ed.), *Central Asia and the Caucasus after the Soviet Union:
    Domestic and International Dynamics* (Gainesville, FL: University Press of
    Florida, 1994), pp. 268–319; S.T. Hunter, *The Transcaucasus in
    Transition: Nation-building and Conflict* (Washington, DC: Center for
    Strategic and International Studies, 1994), pp. 142–51; W.E. Odom and

R. Dujarric, *Commonwealth or Empire? Russia, Central Asia and the Transcaucasus* (Indianapolis, IN: Hudson Institute, 1995), pp. 8–46.

16 On Turkish policy see: S.T. Hunter, *The Transcaucasus in Transition*, pp. 161–70; K. Karpat, 'The Role of Turkey and Iran in Incorporating the Former Soviet Republics into the World System', in K. Dawisha (ed.), *The International Dimensions of Post-Communist Transitions in Russia and the New States of Eurasia* (Armonk, NY: M.E. Sharpe, *The International Politics of Eurasia*, Vol. 10, 1997), pp. 168–96; P. Robins, 'Between Sentiment and Self-Interest: Turkey's Policy Towards Azerbaijan and the Central Asian States', *Middle East Journal* (47/4, 1993), pp. 593–610; A. Ehteshami and E.C. Murphy, 'The Non-Arab Middle East States and the Caucasian/Central Asian Republics: Turkey', *International Relations* (11/6, 1993), pp. 513–31; S. Bolukbashi, 'Ankara's Baku-Centred Transcaucasia Policy: Has It Failed?', *Middle East Journal* (51/1, 1997), pp. 80–94.

17 On Iranian policy see: Hunter, *The Transcaucasus in Transition*, pp. 170–6; Karpat, 'The Role of Turkey and Iran'; E. Herzig, *Iran and the Former Soviet South* (London: RIIA, 1995); G. Winrow, 'Azerbaijan and Iran', in Alvin Z. Rubinstein and Oles M. Smolansky (eds), *Regional Power Rivalries in the New Eurasia* (Armonk, NY: M.E. Sharpe, 1995), pp. 93–111; A. Ehteshami and E.C. Murphy, 'The Non-Arab Middle East States and the Caucasian/Central Asian Republics: Iran and Israel', *International Relations* (12/1, 1994), pp. 81–107; J. Calabrese, 'Iran and Her Northern Neighbours at the Crossroads', *Central Asia Monitor* (1994), Part 1, No. 5, pp. 27–30, Part 2, No. 6, pp. 13–18.

18 R. Motika, 'Probable Iranian Reactions to an Active EU Policy in Caucasia' (Conflict Prevention Network Paper, Stiftung Wissenschaft und Politik, Ebenhausen, 1997), p. 6.

19 On US and European policy see: Hunter, *The Transcaucasus in Transition*, pp. 157–61; Forsythe, *The Politics of Oil in the Caucasus and Central Asia: Problems, Prospects and Policy*, pp. 17–21, 28–29; F.S. Starr, 'Power Failure: American Policy in the Caspian', *National Interest* (47, 1997), pp. 20–32; S.N. MacFarlane, 'A Role for the EU in Preventing Ethnic Conflict' (Conflict Prevention Network Paper, Stiftung Wissenschaft und Politik, Ebenhausen, 1997). For official statements and comments on US policy see: J. Collins in the Hearing of the US Commission on Security and Cooperation in Europe, *Russia and Its Neighbours*, 24 May 1994 (Washington, DC: US Government Printing Office, 1994), pp. 3–9; S. Talbott, *A Farewell to Flashman: American Policy in the Caucasus and Central Asia*, Address at the Johns Hopkins School of Advanced International Studies, Baltimore, Maryland, 21 July

1997; S. Talbott, *US Policy Toward the Caucasus*, Testimony before the Subcommittee on Foreign Operations of the Senate Appropriations Committee, Washington, DC, 31 March 1998; and E. Sherwood-Randall, 'US Policy in the Caucasus', *Contemporary Caucasus Newsletter*, The Berkeley Program in Soviet and Post-Soviet Studies, (5, 1998), pp. 3–4.

20 Hunter, *The Transcausus in Transition*, pp. 157–8; Starr, 'Power Failure'.

21 *Inside Central Asia* (246, 19–25 October 1998), p. 6, and Talbott, *US Policy Toward the Caucasus*.

Chapter 5: Economy

1 On the legacy of Soviet economic development, see G.E. Schroeder, 'Transcaucasia Since Stalin – the Economic Dimension', in R.G. Suny (ed.), *Transcaucasia, Nationalism, and Social Change: Essays in the History of Armenia, Azerbaijan and Georgia* (Ann Arbor, MI. University of Michigan Press, revised edition, 1996), pp. 461–79.

2 Estimates vary widely, but it is often suggested that around 50 per cent of economic activity takes place in the shadow sector. See UNDP, *Human Development Report: Armenia 1996* (Yerevan: UNDP, 1996), p. 22; *Georgian Economic Trends* (first quarter 1998), pp. 9–10; *Azerbaijan Economic Trends* (July–September 1998), pp. 35–47.

3 On the issue of corruption in transition economies in general, see EBRD, *Transition Report 1997*, Annex 2.1, 'The Level and Pattern of Corruption in Transition Economies', pp. 37–9.

4 UNDP, *Human Development Reports: Georgia 1997* (Tbilisi: UNDP, 1997), p. 12.

5 UN/ECE, *Economic Survey of Europe* (1998, No. 1), 'The Three Caucasian Economies, 1991–97', p. 168.

6 *Armenia Economic Trends* (April–June 1998), p. 7.

7 *Georgian Economic Trends* (First quarter 1998), p. 9.

8 *Azerbaijan Economic Trends* (April–June 1998), p. 19.

9 IMF, *Staff Country Reports,* No. 97/36 *Georgia – Recent Economic Developments* (Washington, DC: IMF, May 1997), p. 29.

10 IMF, *Staff Country Reports*, Washington, DC: IMF, No. 96/118 *Republic of Armenia – Recent Economic Developments and Selected Issues* (November 1996), p. 17; No. 97/36 *Georgia – Recent Economic Developments* p. 28.

11 *Azerbaijan Economic Trends* (April–June 1998), p. 66.

12 UN/ECE, *Economic Survey of Europe*, pp. 175–6.

13 On the banking sector, see ibid., p. 178; IMF, *Staff Country Reports*, No. 96/118 *Republic of Armenia – Recent Economic Developments and*

Selected Issues, pp. 22–8; No. 97/1 *Azerbaijan Republic – Recent Economic Developments,* February 1997, pp. 40–44; *Georgia – Recent Economic Developments,* pp. 33–44. On Kirkorian's initiative see S.H. Ghazarian, 'Mr Kerkorian Goes to Yerevan', *Armenian International Magazine* (August 1998), pp. 16–18.

14 On the privatization debate in Armenia, see A.H. Alexandrian, 'Capital Knows No Borders', *Armenian International Magazine* (August 1998), pp. 34–7.

15 UNDP, *Human Development Reports: Georgia 1997,* pp. 21–2.

16 EBRD, *Transition Report 1997,* p. 150; UN/ECE, *Economic Survey of Europe,* p. 177.

17 EBRD, *Transition Report 1997,* p. 171; UN/ECE, *Economic Survey of Europe,* p. 177; IMF, *Staff Country Report ,* No. 97/36 *Georgia – Recent Economic Developments,* pp. 13–17; *Georgian Economic Trends* (first quarter 1998), pp. 68–76.

18 L. Wiesner, *Plans and Realities of Privatization in Azerbaijan* (London: RIIA, CACP Briefing, forthcoming 1999); UN/ECE, *Economic Survey of Europe,* p. 177; *Azerbaijan Economic Trends,* (April–June 1998), pp. 81–97; IMF, *Staff Country Reports,* No. 97/1 *Azerbaijan Republic – Recent Economic Developments,* pp. 51–5; EBRD, *Transition Report 1997,* p. 152.

19 The data on sectoral development are drawn from UN/ECE, *Economic Survey of Europe,* pp. 180–82; IMF, *Staff Country Reports,* No. 96/118 *Republic of Armenia – Recent Economic Developments and Selected Issues* No. 97/1 *Azerbaijan Republic – Recent Economic Developments;* No. 97/36 *Georgia – Recent Economic Developments* and various issues of *Armenia Economic Trends, Azerbaijan Economic Trends* and *Georgian Economic Trends.*

20 On agriculture in Georgia and Azerbaijan, see World Bank Country Studies, *Armenia: the Challenge of Reform in the Agricultural Sector* and *Georgia: Reform in the Food and Agriculture Sector* (Washington, DC: World Bank, 1996).

21 IMF, *Staff Country Reports,* No. 97/36 *Georgia – Recent Economic Developments,* pp. 17–20, 44–5; *Georgian Economic Trends,* first quarter 1998, 77–80.

22 O. Skagen, *Caspian Gas* (London: RIIA, Former Soviet South Paper, 1997), pp. 26–9.

23 On Azerbaijan's oil industry see R. Ebel, *Energy Choices in the Near Abroad: The Haves and the Have-nots Face the Future* (Washington, DC: Center for Strategic and International Studies, 1997), pp. 34–67;

Azerbaijan Economic Trends (April–June 1998), pp. 25–31.

24 IMF, *Staff Country Reports*, No. 97/1 *Azerbaijan Republic – Recent Economic Developments*, p. 10; International Energy Agency, *Caspian Oil and Gas: The Supply Potential of Central Asia and Transcaucasia* (IEA, 1998), p. 157.

25 World Bank, *Azerbaijan: From Crisis to Sustained Growth* (Washington, DC: World Bank, 1993), pp. 115–34.

26 *Azerbaijan Economic Trends* (April–June 1998), p. 30.

27 G. McDonell, 'The Euro-Asian Corridor', in R. Allison (ed.), *Challenges for the Former Soviet South* (Washington, DC and London: Brookings/ RIIA, 1996), pp. 307–54.

28 Z. Anjaparidze, 'Georgia and the "New Silk Road"', *Prism* (4/14, 10 July 1998); T. Halpin, 'A Road Not So Smooth', *Armenian International Magazine* (October 1998), pp. 16–19.

29 J. Roberts, *Caspian Pipelines*, (London: RIIA, 1996); J. Roberts, *Caspian Pipelines 1999* (London: RIIA, forthcoming 1999); R. Forsythe, *The Politics of Oil in the Caucasus and Central Asia: Problems, Prospects and Policy*, Adelphi Paper 300 (London: International Institute for Strategic Studies, 1996); Ebel, *Energy Choices in the Near Abroad*, pp. 51–66.

30 UN/ECE, *Economic Survey of Europe*, p. 172. The data in this section are drawn primarily from the IMF *Staff Country Reports* and the *Armenia, Azerbaijan* and *Georgian Economic Trends* series.

31 The UNDP *Human Development Reports*: *Georgia 1997, Armenia 1996* and *Azerbaijan 1997* and the *Armenia, Azerbaijan* and *Georgian Economic Trends* series give detailed information on social conditions.

32 M. Kurkchiyan, *Healthcare in Armenia: The Human Cost of Transition* (London: RIIA, CACP Briefing, No. 16, March 1998).

33 UNDP, *Human Development Report 1997* (Oxford: OUP, 1997).

34 J. Hughes et al., 'Karabakh Lives', *Armenian International Magazine* (October 1998), pp. 20–33.

Further reading

Of the works cited in the notes, the following are recommended for further reading by those wishing to explore specific issues in greater depth:

Allison, R. (ed.), *Challenges for the Former Soviet South* (Washington, DC: Brookings/RIIA, 1996).

Allison, R. and C. Bluth (eds), *Security Dilemmas in Russia and Eurasia* (RIIA, 1998).

Aves, J., *Georgia: from Chaos to Stability?* (London: RIIA, 1996).

Baev, P., *Russia's Policies in the Caucasus* (London: RIIA, 1997).

Coppieters, B. (ed.), *Contested Borders in the Caucasus* (Brussels: VUB Press, 1996).

Coppieters, B., G. Nodia and Y. Andchabadze (eds), *Georgians and Abkhazians: The Search for a Peace Settlement* (Cologne: Bundesinstitut für ostwissenschaftliche und internationale Studien, 1998).

Curtis, G. E. (ed.), *Armenia, Azerbaijan and Georgia: Country Studies* (Washington, DC: Library of Congress, 1995).

Dawisha, A. & K. (eds), *The Making of Foreign Policy in Russia and the New States of Eurasia* (Armonk, NY: M.E. Sharpe, *The International Politics of Eurasia*, Vol. 4, 1995).

Dawisha, K. and B. Parrot (eds), *Conflict, Cleavage and Change in Central Asia and the Caucasus* (Cambridge: CUP, 1997).

Gachechiladze, R., *The New Georgia: Space, Society, Politics* (London: UCL Press, 1995).

Hunter, S.T., *The Transcaucasus in Transition: Nation-Building and Conflict* (Washington, DC: Center for Strategic and International Studies, 1994).

Further reading

Masih, J.R. and R.O. Krikorian, *Armenia at the Crossroads* (Amsterdam: Harwood Academic Publishers, forthcoming 1999).

Suny, R.G. (ed.), *Transcaucasia, Nationalism, and Social Change: Essays in the History of Armenia, Azerbaijan and Georgia* (Ann Arbor: University of Michigan Press, revised edition 1996).

Walker, E.W., *No Peace, No War in the Caucasus: Secessionist Conflict in Chechnya, Abkhazia, and Nagorno-Karabakh* (Cambridge, MA: Harvard University, John F. Kennedy School of Government, Strengthening Democratic Institutions Project, 1998).

Wright, J.F.R., S. Goldenberg and R. Schofield (eds), *Transcaucasian Boundaries* (London: UCL Press, 1996).

The following journals regularly contain articles or news on the Caucasus (URLs are given for those publications that may be accessed exclusively or more readily via the Internet):

Armenian International Magazine.
Azerbaijan International (http://www.azer.com/).
Caucasian Regional Studies (http://poli.vub.ac.be/publi).
Central Asian Survey.
Inside Central Asia.
The TransCaucasus: A Chronology (http://www.soros.org/caucasus/).

On economic and social development, the following publications contain detailed information and analysis:

EBRD, the annual *Transition Report* and *Transition Report Update*.

IMF, *Staff Country Reports* (Washington DC: IMF); in particular No. 96/118 *Republic of Armenia – Recent Economic Developments and Selected Issues* (November 1996); No. 97/1 *Azerbaijan Republic – Recent Economic Developments* (February 1997); No. 97/36 *Georgia – Recent Economic Developments* (May 1997).

UN/ECE, *Economic Survey of Europe*; in particular No. 1, 1998, Chapter 4, 'The Three Caucasian Economies, 1991–97', pp. 165–86.

UNDP, *Human Development Reports* Georgia 1997, Armenia 1996, Azerbaijan 1996.

World Bank, *Statistical Handbook: States of the Former USSR* and other reports.

Particularly useful are the monthly and quarterly publications supported by the Tacis programme of the European Union: